Mark \

YOU

Universal Lesson for Change

& Reclaiming Your Power

MARK WOOD

ISBN 9798358731202

Independently Published

Note on the Author

Mark has been working in the mental health system for twenty years, where he has used his own life experiences to help others.

Mark lived a destructive lifestyle for much of his adolescant life, using alcohol and drugs to mask what was really going on for him.

His real life experiences have given Mark a firm foundation that wasn't just created from studying others experiences, but in the reality of a sometimes cruel world.

This book is an amalgamation of his life, the universal lessons that allowed him to let go and the decades of experience helping others to become the version of themselves they wanted to be.

Thanks to Karen my angel and rock, couldn't have

done it without your constant support.

Contents

Om is a remarkably simple sound

with a complex meaning. It is the

whole universe coalesced into a

single word, representing the

union of mind, body, and spirit.

YOU

Introduction

I could not stop; I am not even sure that I wanted to stop.

Blow after blow, punch after punch, raining down on this bloke's head. Every time his head bounced back up off the hard pavement, I would relentlessly punch it back down

People speak of a red mist coming over them when they lose their shit; there was no red mist that night: I knew exactly what I was doing. This was the most powerful I had ever felt, the anger that had been running through my veins for so long was finally being freed.

This was not my first scrap, but it was the first time I had taken it to this level of violence.

My sister came out of the pub. 'Mark, what are you

doing?' she screamed.

Even that wasn't enough to stop the barrage of violence.

'Go back in the pub, Sis,' I told her calmly, and she did.

Then I returned to the onslaught against the man unfortunate enough to be at the end of my anger; an anger I was not sure I wanted to control in that moment.

I am not sure I would ever have stopped if the blue flashing lights of a police car had not come into my peripheral vision, this was enough for the flight reflex to kick in. Looking back, my whole life could have turned out differently if I hadn't noticed the lights; I could have killed him.

I ran back up into the pub, where my mates saw my blood-spattered shirt.

"The police have just pulled up," I exclaimed, breathless from the run up the stairs.

"Woody, get under the pool table and keep quiet," a couple of my mates shouted out.

Five minutes later the police walked in. "Has someone just run in here with a bloody, white shirt?"

I heard a couple of mates say, "No Officer, no one has come in here."

As I had dragged the fight away from the pub, they could not be a hundred percent sure I was there or whether I had run down Recreation Road. My mates were walking around the pool table playing pool as naturally as you like, as if there was nothing out of the ordinary going on.

Then there was me, laid there, scared. I wasn't scared of getting caught; I wasn't scared of any repercussions from the bloke. I feared *me*. All of the years of fearing everybody else, and now I had molded who I was into someone that scared me.

This book is for grownups. There will be swearing, tales of laughter, and tears of joy and sadness. But if you are stuck in a rut and are going around in circles, then this book will teach you how to find YOU, the real YOU, the YOU that you dream of, being free from the restraints of your past and the fears for your future.

I have been guiding and teaching people to become the best version of themselves for twenty years, a journey that has seen me work in care homes, homeless hostels, young people's homes, private counselling practice, teaching meditation and mindfulness and starting a mental health project working with adults and young people in a woodland setting.

I have written a book that people can connect to; it is about how I became the boss of the negative beliefs that had been programmed into me from a young age.

I have read too many books when doing my counselling training and when looking into spiritualism that left me frustrated at the all-knowing language of the authors. This will not be like that; it is an honest account of a flawed man who is searching for more.

Before I go any further, I want to say that I am just an ordinary guy I don't live in a cave at the top of a mountain, with my legs crossed twenty-three hours a day chanting Om, hoping to find Nirvana. I have been known to swear, eat too much and occasionally am partial to a pint or two!

The recollections of my past are my memories, so they may well differ from other people who were around me. This is fine, as memories are made up of your interpretation of that time.

It has been a journey that took me from an angry, naïve, and conflicted young man beating the crap out of someone, to the man I am today.

I have seen people make miraculous transformations in their lives over the years, and I believe more people could benefit from the chance to change. This book aims to instill the same sense of belief in YOU that my clients have in themselves after implementing the lessons I have taught, allowing YOU to become the version of YOU that YOU deserve to be.

Blimey that is a lot of YOU, but YOU know what? It's time that YOU concentrated on the miracle that YOU are. YOU are one of a kind, there's not another YOU on the planet - fanbloodytastic I reckon.!

The book will teach you how to let go of and accept the negative influences that have impacted your life to this point, gain control of the programmed thoughts and behaviours that you carry on your shoulders every day. Your history can keep you in negative thought and behaviour patterns, hold you back from putting you first, and stops you from taking a gamble on your own happiness.

The book covers thirteen universal lessons. The universal lesson is outlined at the start of each chapter, followed by a recollection of an experience I had personally that cemented that lesson. Finally, at the end of each chapter, there will be a tip around following the lessons spoken about in the chapter, a task connected to the topic, plus further reading recommendations.

I would love for you to use this book as a friend, something you can connect to and keep going back to for advice when needed.

So please write in the book, highlight areas that really make an impact whilst you read, write your thoughts in the margins. Let the book become part of the foundation for who you become, a friend you can rely on when you are not putting in place all the things you will learn along the way.

If your shoulders are heavy with the burden of your past, or your head is full of doubt for your future then this book will teach you how to learn from both and make the moment you are in glorious.

Universal Lesson #1

You must take risks if you want your life to

change.

Taking risks and living outside the box makes you feel alive and helps build trust in yourself. It is like finding a key to the shackles that have restricted your freedom and can create a sense of excitement about the world around you.

Only you can change your own path, it is not for anyone else to make your life choices. If you want your life, or parts of it to be different, then you must make changes. Step out of your safety bubble and give yourself permission to create the kind of world – internal and external – that you want to be in.

We all have the right to reach for the stars, no matter what has come before. The only limits in life are the ones we put on ourselves.

Finding your true self will make these limits evaporate, giving you the control and power to create anything you wish.

For years I had been having thoughts around giving it all up and going travelling, but it never came to fruition, mainly because of my anxieties and fears. But in the summer of 2013, it was engulfing every free moment of thought, leaving me feeling it was now or never: I was not getting any younger.

Even if I was in my fortieth year, I wasn't going through a midlife crisis. Not once did I consider getting a motorbike and shiny new leathers, mainly because my mate scared the life out of me once when I jumped on the back of his bike to go for a game of badminton.

He had one of these super bikes, a seven-fifty something or other, but I trusted him to keep me safe. To his word he took it nice and steady leaving the village, then we reached London Beach Road. When you are walking home drunk this stretch of road seems like it never ends, and on more than one occasion I have given up the walk and laid on the side of it for a kip, before waking up a few hours later to finish off the journey, hungover from too much beer and feeling damp with the morning dew.

When he reached this part of the road, without warning he turned heavily on the throttle. Well fuck me, I thought I was going to fly off the back, only to be run over by the cars following. So, I did what all manly men do in these moments, and I wrapped my arms around him, as if he were the love of my life!

I had a midlife awakening, not a crisis at all. I saw it as me realising that there could be more to life. The word crisis is used towards people in their later years who, out of the blue, decide to make changes to their lives. I don't agree with it.

I had, without realising, been following the norm for years, living a life by rules and expectations that I hadn't even noticed. In my late thirties something started to change; there must be more to life than working my socks off to earn money that I wasted on shed loads of possessions (half of which I never touched) just to look right.

Suddenly, all the things I had never done because they went against the grain of society, family expectations and my programming, became important. I wanted to push my boundaries.

My life was good in 2013, I had my private counselling business, I had a nice little house all to myself, I had amazing family and friends and a little bit of cash in the bank.
But there was something missing amongst it all, there was no adventure, no challenge.

There was also the risk of me falling back into old

habits from my twenties. I was spending a lot of time on my own. Many a night I sat in with a few bottles of cheap vino getting pissed, feeling sorry for myself. It was an old behaviour that had previously led to a dark, dark place. I did not want to go there again. I had lost my purpose. When I start to feel lonely, even when I am surrounded by people who love me, it's time to make a change.

It was all a bit comfortable and easy; I felt I wasn't being tested in my life. Days and weeks would disappear with nothing valuable to talk about, except for the amazing changes my clients were making in their own lives.

I was lost, lonely and fading away into nothingness. There had to be more to my life, it felt like I was drifting through space.

I realised I was desperate to let go of or become friendlier with my own past and stop using others as a way of not fulfilling my own internal happiness.

I was jealous of my clients; this revelation came out of

the blue and I was not overly comfortable with it at first.

Every week a client would come to a session and explain to me the new things they had tried, how they had started a hobby that they used to do twenty years ago, how the sessions were transforming their lives.

I felt humbled that I could be part of these changes, that these amazing people who were going through all sorts of trauma, abuse and self-defeating behaviours found the strength to step back and make changes. It was the exact reason why I trained to become a counsellor, so I could make a difference.

I wanted to give myself the same opportunity to heal. I wanted to give myself the same importance that I was giving everyone else.

It would be nice to gain some freedom from the shit I still carried, and I felt certain that this would be achieved by travelling, meeting strangers, and experiencing new cultures. Travelling had been my constant go to for years when thinking about making a big change.

So here I was in the summer of 2013 with a choice to make, give it all up for the unknown or carry on as I was.

I was full of fear and anxiety over this choice. I felt I had to get it right first time or it would not work out. There was also the niggling thought that I was too fat, too old, and too set in my ways to make the most of the experience. I was holding back from making the final decision to leave it all behind, nervous of making myself look a fool.

What if I could find a way of lessening my fear? What if there was a way I could manage the risk? I started to look at volunteering experiences for a set period, thinking this would be a great way of testing whether going to a strange country and being in an unfamiliar environment was really what I was looking for.

I was going to have a taster session; I was going to dip my toe in the water and see how it felt, then make my big decision depending on the outcome. This took away some of the pressure; I could just go and have an amazing experience without the burden of it having to tick all the boxes.

I found an amazing company called *Education & Health Nepal* (EHN), which was run by two English blokes who had themselves taken risks to do something amazing. One of them lived in London and organised this side of it, the other fella had moved to Kathmandu and ran the organising of all the volunteers.

I spoke to them and organised a six-week trip to Nepal, where the first two to three weeks would be spent living in the hills with a Nepalese family, then I would have three to four weeks travelling around Nepal.

I am not sure why I chose Nepal, but once I had come across the EHN website my instinct leapt in joy, telling me it was the right choice.

I knew I wanted the whole experience to push my limits, to test my metal in a situation that was the opposite of my nice comfortable life. What would do that more than living in a tiny home in the far-off hills of Nepal, having to

farm whatever you want to eat, no supermarkets within miles

and weather that I knew would make me uncomfortable in

my own skin?

I have got to tell you, I felt alive. For the first time in

ages, I had excitement flowing through my veins. It was like I

had been jump-started after my battery had gone flat.

It was one of the biggest risks I had taken in my life so

far. I was full of questions that could not be answered. Would

this change my life? Would it be all I imagined it to be? Would

I have another huge decision to make by the end of it?

I did not care that the answers were not available to

me; that was all part of it.

Taking these risks is going to scare the shite out of you,

your auto pilot responses will constantly try and pull you

back to old safe behaviours.

The first choice you must make in this journey is

whether you want the rest of your life to continue as it is, or do you want parts of it to change. This is the start of all heroic journeys since time has begun, shall I stand up to my demons or shall I continue to let them direct my life?

It is not easy, there will be bumps in the road, you will desperately, at times, want to stop walking this new path to return to the old.

But what I can promise you is this, if you stick to your journey of discovery and change, the life ahead of you can be truly magical.

Tip for everyday-

You do not have to go to the extremes I did to take a risk; there are opportunities within everyday life. Say hello to the person you feel connected to, ask for the promotion you feel you deserve, sign up for the training course that caught your eye, try a hobby you have been thinking about for ages, change jobs if your present one is draining the joy out of you, make your passions in life more central to your every day.

The secret to taking risks and leaps of faith is not getting wrapped up in the future. Have faith that wherever it takes you is where you are meant to be.

Task-

I want you to buy a journal, they are a fantastic way of recording your journey. It may feel strange to start with and you will overthink what you are writing at times, this is natural, just go with the flow. Your journal will evolve with you, how you use it is up to you.

Use colours, pictures, write at angles or on the lines. Whatever works for you, this journal should reflect your personality and your journey.

On the first page draw three columns. In the first, make a list of things you dream of doing and things you want to be different. In the second column write down the barriers that are holding you back, then in a third column list the things you could do to achieve them.

Further reading- Take some time to read *Pathways to Bliss by* Joseph Campbell. Joseph made the connection between the myths and stories we hear growing up and our own lives, saying that we are all on similar heroes' journeys to find our bliss. Immensely powerful and informative, it will help you connect to your own journey.

Universal Lesson #2

Become aware of the lessons your critical voice

is trying to teach you.

My critical voice is a pain in the arse and has been for most of my life because I have fed it with thoughts and behaviours that it grasps onto like a vice.

It turns out that my critical voice was trying to teach me lessons, the universe was telling me to take notice of what it was saying. Every aspect of our lives is an opportunity to learn, the critical voice is no different.

Becoming aware of your critical voice and your own self-talk in general will help you make changes. The language we use reflects our thoughts. **If you can grow the awareness of the language you are using, you can change your thoughts and as our internal and external world is created by our thoughts, it is a fantastic weapon to have in your armory.**

If you want to see yourself and the world you are in differently, speak to yourself differently.

By making the decision to go to Nepal I had opened a doorway for my critical mind to go bat-shit crazy, which it did with gusto the week leading up to me going.

Leaving was a rollercoaster of emotions, from fear and anxiety to anticipation and exhilaration. I felt uncomfortable with the idea of putting myself first.

Who would have thought that would be a barrier? Guilt racked every bone in my body. How could I leave my family and clients? Who would look after them?

Then the old obsession with 'what if' appeared. What if

all my clients fucked off while I was away? How would I pay my bills? What if something bad happened to someone, how I would I cope with not being there to rescue them? What if I hated it and wanted to come home after a week? What if I loved it and didn't want to come back at all? What if a nuclear bomb went off and there was no England to return to? You know, that sort of stuff.

Our minds can be a proper pain in the backside sometimes.

As soon as I got off the plane the heat hit me like a hammer. Phil from EHN met me at the airport and took me to the little hotel I would stay in for a couple of days before leaving to meet the family in the mountains. I had made it.

Within hours I was thinking that I should have chosen a cooler place to dip my toes into a life-changing experience, Kathmandu is a furnace.

I am not a big fan of mega heat, twenty-four to twenty-five degrees is about the limit for me, not another ten or fifteen degrees on top of that. Still, it was too late to redirect to Sweden, so onwards and upwards.

I hated Kathmandu over those first couple of days, it was too hot, too dusty, too many people, no one had any manners, and I was always surrounded by buildings.

The only thing I enjoyed over those first couple of days was my morning cuppa and ciggy whilst watching the locals play badminton. At seven each morning I went out to the balcony that surrounded the hotel watched these amazing athletes, just ordinary guys that met every morning to play before work. It was quite a sight, and at least I started the day with a smile.

I found myself full of regret. Kathmandu was sapping any excitement I had. It was a barrage on the senses, but not in a good way. I felt overwhelmed every waking moment; it was as if Kathmandu was a heavy-weight boxer knocking me back down onto the canvas every time I tried to think positively. I felt battered and bruised.

The first full day I was there a guide took me on a tour of the city. I did not take in any of the tour; I spent the whole day wanting to be back in my hotel room, hiding away from the reality of the situation I had put myself in for the next six weeks. I felt shit. What had I done? I had no interest in the imposing temples, the locals trying to flog me stuff I did not want, the new food or the guide's informative explanations, poor girl.

I spent the hours after the tour hiding in my room certain that I was not built for travelling. I was too old, too fat and too unfit.

I had closed myself off from noticing any of it, as the tour earlier had proved. All the other volunteers seemed to be relishing the whole experience, but I couldn't find any enthusiasm. I felt like a right pillock.

I was racked with doubt and guilt, hiding in my room that night. I was hyper critical of my choices that had brought me to this moment. If someone had offered me a way home that night I would have gone, I did not want to spend any more time with my inner voices beating the shit out of me.

I needed to move on. I felt drained emotionally and physically.

The night before travelling to the homestay I had a meeting with Phil from EHN, so he could give me some pointers and encouragement.

Phil explained to me in his permanently jovial voice, 'I'll take you to the bus station and from there you'll go to the end of the line, where you'll be met by the father of the family.'

'I can do that,' I said in my most invented confident voice.

Phil then pointed out, 'There's a leisurely walk of a couple of hours until you reach their home, where they will help you settle in.'

'I can handle a short walk. I enjoy walking.' Although

in my head I was saying *I enjoy walking in normal temperatures, this could be something different all together.*

As the meeting came to an end Phil imparted his final piece of advice: 'They eat huge amounts and will expect you to need the same amount to survive. *Pugyo* means I am full in Nepalese. Don't forget it, it's the most important word you'll need for the three weeks.'

'I can't see that being a problem, Phil. I like my food, as you can see,' I replied without a hint at the anger I felt towards myself for drawing attention to my weight.

I spent four hours on a rickety old bus, surrounded by old guys who were coughing so much I thought their lungs were going to jump out of their mouths and make a run for it.

The driver of said bus was a lunatic, which I found out later was a common trait among bus drivers. The roads were like dirt tracks and there were potholes the size of small continents that would throw you out of your seat at regular intervals. The buses are not designed for people who are six foot one, and I had a bruise on my forehead from headbutting the window and ceiling for four hours.

My internal dialogue was unsurprisingly having a field day.

What the bloody hell was I doing?

I was finding it hard to embrace the moment. On the left was a cliff edge and each time another bus passed in the opposite direction there was a millimetre gap between us. I was not having fun and the doubts of Kathmandu just continued.

This whole trip was going to be a bloody nightmare. What was I thinking? What an idiot for leaving my comfort behind.

These were just a few of the derogatory thoughts spiraling through my mind.

We stopped halfway through the journey for a drink and food stop. For me this was fifteen minutes to smoke as many cigarettes as I could and have a little chat with myself. The first three days of what should have been a huge adventure had turned into an emotional nightmare, where I could not stop criticising myself for making such a stupid decision.

It was time for me to pull up my big boy pants and embrace where I was and start to learn lessons from this quest.

The next two hours on the bus were still bloody scary but I revelled in it, I remember saying to myself, 'it's not your time to die yet so enjoy it.'

I started to believe that I was exactly where I was meant to be, which enabled me to lose some of the doubt.

This only changed because I consciously changed how I was talking to myself, which meant my experience of exactly the same situation changed.

We arrived at Trishuli at midday. Yes, that's right, bang in the middle of the day. Luckily, it was only about forty degrees, so I did not feel too hot for someone who weighs eighteen stone.

I jumped off the bus, well actually I gingerly lowered myself to the ground. As soon as my foot touched the floor, I was grabbed by the head of the family I would be staying with and we were off to his home with his son who had come along for the walk.

I had never travelled like this before, so I had brought the kitchen sink with me and my rucksack weighed about twenty-five kilos.

I want to remind you of what Phil said before I left. *It's a nice easy, short walk.*

Lying bastard!

I can tell you, before I even reached the bottom of the hill where their home was, I was half baked and breathing out of my backside. It was so hot, but the father and son were walking along as if they were on roller skates. And not showing any interest in my lack of fitness or the fact I was falling behind already. To be fair I was forty years old so should be able to look after myself.

It got worse. By halfway up the hill-stroke-bloody-mountain I started to get cramp on the inside of both thighs. If this has never happened to you then you won't understand, but I thought I was going to die.

'Why don't we take a shorter route?' the father said as he could see I was struggling. (Not sure how, I was sure I was hiding it so well.)

'If you think that's a good idea,' I replied, trying to hide my joy at the fact there was a quicker route, but also thinking to myself, why the bloody hell didn't we start off by taking the short route? Maybe they were trying to give me a baptism of fire into what their lives were like; personally I would have liked a gentler introduction.

With a knowing grin on his face the father said, 'This way will be better.'

This route may have been shorter, but it was definitely

not better. At points I was on my knees dragging myself up inclines that threatened me with slipping right back down to where I had started.

Four and a half hours later we arrived. I had cramp in both legs and could hardly walk. I was dehydrated, sunburnt and my lungs were making a run for it.

We walked around the corner of his home to be greeted by about a dozen people, all smiling and happy to see me. I was struggling to put one leg in front of another and I was sure I looked a proper Brit abroad with my beer belly and sunburnt face. I hid all my pain, put a big smile on my face and got introduced to each person individually. Everyone was so happy to meet me, and I selfishly could only think about being anywhere but there, preferably lying down.

They showed me where I would be sleeping so that I could put my bag down and was told to come out when I was ready. As soon as the door closed, I fell on the bed in agony and tried to compose myself, drink some water and get my head in the game.

My head was a mess of emotions at this point. I was concerned about the impression I had made; I was worried about how I was going to cope with this experience, I was physically worn out and had only been in Nepal three days, but most of all I was hyper critical of myself for being so fucking stupid. How did I ever think I was the right person for this kind of experience?

It was at this point that I realised that the window next to my bed looked through into the lean-to that the goats and cow lived in. The sound of animals peeing and shitting next to my ears became part of the music I would fall asleep to for the next three weeks. It did eventually become quite soothing, with the steady flow of the animal's daily outpourings comforting me to sleep.

Fifteen minutes later I walked out of my bedroom to join the group, who seemed fascinated by me.

'You want shower?' I was asked by someone.

I was shocked. How could they have a shower halfway up this mountain? But I went with it anyway.

The shower was up on a little hill at the back of the two houses, so I had a bit of privacy away from the front yard of their homes. I have to say I was a little disappointed when I found it. It was not a nice cubicle with a space for your shower gel and sponge. In reality, it was a hosepipe attached to a lump of concrete with a tap. The hosepipe was run through the mountain stream and water would spurt out of the nozzle, ingenious really.

I was hot and bothered so armed with my towel and soap I decided to have a shower, with the company of some bloody huge spiders. It was quite nice showering alfresco; the view was amazing. Between the jungle canopy, I could see the huge steps that were the rice fields, leading to the valley at the bottom of the mountains where I had started my body-sapping walk all those hours before.

There was a slight covering of cloud, which just added

a sense of loftiness, I felt like I was on top of the world. It was so green, so many different shades of one colour and rolling hills of green carpet. It looked like you could walk back down on top of the trees, it was such a welcoming, soft blanket of green.

I was just getting comfortable with showering out in the open when I turned around and saw a group of the locals watching me; that was not odd or disconcerting at all! Then one of the young boys came up to me.

'Why are you so fat?'

Wallop. That was my ten minutes of quiet mind obliterated: on came the onslaught of negative thoughts that had encased me for the first three days of this adventure.

Needless to say, the rest of my shower was cut short, and how the fuck was I going to shower over the next three weeks if I was going to get insulted by some little fucker every time I got out my soap?

As we sat crossed legged in their clay home for our first

meal that evening, my first opportunity to use pugyo came around.

When they served the dinner plates, I was astounded by the amount of rice on them, it looked enough to feed a family of ten, not just me. I ate what must have been a quarter of the plate before I was stuffed. You should have seen their faces when I said pugyo , it was as if I had said I was a woman and my name is Maria. It was pure shock. I could hear their internal voices going *how can a man that size be full up so quickly? He has hardly touched it.* But after repeating myself half a dozen times they got that I might honestly be full.

After the meal which, even though huge, tasted bloody good, they could see I was knackered, so they took me to my room.

The walls of the bedroom were covered with old newspaper, I never asked why but I'm guessing as some sort of insulation. The bed itself was covered with brightly coloured blankets. It looked inviting after the long exhausting day I'd had.

As I got undressed to get under the cover of my holey mosquito net (seriously I could have fitted my head through some of the holes) I saw a spider on the wall at the end of my bed. *Oh, my fucking god, it is huge.* I am pretty sure it smiled and winked at me as I gingerly manoeuvred under cover hoping not to disturb it!

The bed was rock hard, but I was shattered, so it did not take me long to drift off into a dreamless sleep.

That story just goes to show the power and the distracting influence of our language. Becoming conscious of the words we use towards ourselves is so important to changing yourself and the world you create around you.

I had spent so much time in my life allowing my critical voice lots of space. I had not even considered that if I learnt to sit with it and learn from what it was trying to tell me I could make massive changes.

Whenever I caught my negative language, it just made me angry with myself, which fed into the belief that I was an angry man and that an angry man did not need to be vulnerable, because my anger protected me from everything bad.

Our language keeps us in a behaviour and thought cycle that has been imprinted through our life's experience; this can only be understood by learning the history of our negative thinking.

As in the last chapter, sit with the fear, learn from it, and then move forward to change it.

Tip for every day-

Without awareness of your negative self-talk, it will only ever have a negative impact on you, but if used as a tool for your benefit it can really help you let go of stuff you may have been carrying for a long time. It can teach you to problem solve, be honest with yourself and help you gain a better understanding of your triggers to negative behaviour patterns.

The secret to becoming the boss of your critical voice is to become conscious of it. Not to follow it down negative paths of thoughts and behaviours, but to welcome it in with an eagerness to learn from it.

It takes time to re-programme so don't get disheartened if it takes a while for new habits to form. All these lessons are about raising your awareness and supporting you to live a more conscious life.

Task-

Start to use reflection as a conscious tool to help grow your awareness. Take ten minutes at the end of each day to sit, just sit in silence with yourself. Ask yourself these questions- was I unkind to myself today? Did my language make me feel rubbish at any point today? What triggered my negative language? What could I do differently next time?

Don't forget to put this in your journal; you will go back to it as part of your journey I promise.

Further Reading-

There are two books that I found extremely powerful when I read them, they are both about people who stepped out of their comfort zone to try and become friendlier with their pasts and create something new. They are *Eat, Pray, Love* by Elizabeth Gilbert and *Wild* by Cheryl Strayed.

Universal Lesson #3

You have a choice over how the rest of your

story is written.

The way we see ourselves and the world around us gets programmed into us from our first breath, we become creations of what we experience. Our parents create our personality traits and views of the world based on their own history; we are then given into the hands of teachers who mold you into what they expect a student is meant to be. Then as you get older peer influence comes into the equation alongside media, leaving us in our late teens with a storyline that our subconscious mind believes it must follow.

This grows an auto pilot response to thoughts, situations, and people. All of this happens without us having much control over what goes in and what doesn't, until you get to an age when you start to think for yourself, then the opportunity for changing some of the programming arises.

We have been given an amazing tool in our minds, so try and use it. If negative thoughts and behaviours can be programmed in us, that means the programmes can be re-mastered. Do not believe that because something has always been a particular way that it always must be. Just because you think it doesn't make it true.

The universal lesson here is you have a choice. Believing you have a choice is the hard part, but you most definitely do have a choice over how you feel and how you behave.

My first few years on the planet were full of joy within a family that could not have been any closer, we spent time together, went on holiday, had Sunday teatime full of crumpets and Sunday night TV (which was something to get excited about in those days).

Then I started primary school: what a shock to the system that was for a shy five-year-old.

As soon as I started primary, I became the victim of the school bully. There was name calling, little jabs to a variety of areas on my body and derogatory comments. I felt so weak and scared.

I would sit on my own at break thinking, why me? Although deep down I knew why, but it was easier to dismiss the reasons than to admit to them.

My dad was the bobby in a little village in Kent called Woodchurch, which is where I started primary school. I was five and I thought my dad was a hero, I still do. So, when I started to get bullied because of his job, I just didn't understand what was going on.

It's amazing how powerful words can be and before I knew it, I had adopted a couple of new names, Piglet (the offspring of a pig(policeman) and Goofy (I could fit my thumb between my top and bottom rows of teeth). My dad was called all sorts of things, but I was not brave enough to stick up for him. Can you imagine a five-year-old feeling guilty for not being brave enough to stand up for his dad? It was not a great feeling.

I was left feeling as if I was different to the other kids, that I was not made the same as them. I did not see anyone else getting bullied, so it must have been down to me. That feeling of being different has never left me, but now I embrace it rather than fear it. Now I don't want to be like everyone else, but as a kid all I wanted to do was fit in.

I didn't want my dad knowing what was happening so I kept it to myself, although at some point it got found out, my memory does not recall how. This is when my parents moved me to a new school and I managed to get a couple of years' respite.

But the scars had been scratched into my young mind by then, forming an internal dialogue surrounding the type of kid I was. Externally I presented as a shy, kind and loving kid, but internally I was lost and lonely.

I do remember a time at the new school when I stood in the centre circle of the playground, and me and one of the tough kids stood there taking it in turns to kick each other in the shins as a competition to see who would back down first. Seems a daft thing to do now, but it helped me, because I never got bullied at that school, even after wetting myself during my cycling proficiency test (yes it was as devastating as it sounds!). I will not even mention the fact that the only spare pair of trousers in the lost property were a purple pair of cords, which obviously helped me blend in for the rest of the day. I mean it hardly got noticed at all, honest!

But I was quite resilient by this point and the whole embarrassing spectacle got forgotten very quickly.

I saw out my last couple of years at primary school without any other memorable events, just a normal kid doing normal things.

Being eleven is a strange age because suddenly you think you are a grown up and that you have rights and can do whatever you like. This was not the case and once I realised this, I became a stroppy teenager pushing the boundaries.

My poor parents had the three of us pushing boundaries all at the same time, bless them. I imagine it must have been a bloody nightmare.

This was the age I first became aware that I noticed things: people's faces, how words were said, how people interacted, understanding the things that were not said aloud and my instinct for things happening.

I had two things going on during this period in my life, the first was my parent's relationship was changing for the worse and I could see it happening despite them trying to hide it.

The other is that I came across my friendly bully again in secondary school, which also led to other kids seeing me as an easy target.

I was being bullied virtually every day during school and it also extended to the long, lonely mile walk home.

I spent the next three years learning how to put on a mask. I imagined the last thing my parents needed to see was their little boy messed up emotionally because other kids enjoyed pushing me, trashing my school bag, punching me in the back and calling me cruel names.

I would hear them from behind me walking home, 'Oi piggy fucking come here!'

I tried to ignore it, hoping they would get bored and leave me alone. But why would that day be any different to any others? This was my lot; I just had to learn how to carry on.

Then would come the hard push in the back. 'Leave me alone. I haven't done anything,' I would squeak out knowing it would not make any difference.

For the rest of the walk home I would receive a barrage of insults, punches, and attempts at tripping me up.

Just before I walked in my front door I would dig deep and my happy face got put on, I was like a child Worzel Gummidge with a head for every occasion. I would walk through the back door where my mum in her usual cheerful voice would welcome me with 'How was your day, Son?' I would reply, 'Been good thanks. Just going up stairs to sort my bag out.'

Once in my room, the façade would drop and I would cry into my pillow for five minutes, making sure to keep it quiet so no one would hear.

This was the first time in my life that I learnt that wearing a mask is a great way of hiding sadness and loneliness. It was not even to protect me; it was to protect the people around me from knowing their son was not happy.

When I was about twelve, things started to change at home. I was picking up hidden signs every day.

I felt like I was on my own seeing these small changes, little things like the laughter that had filled the family home since childhood starting to seep out of the walls, leaving an uncertain atmosphere covering everything in the house. The natural smiles of my parents turned into forced smiles, you know the ones - where you can see the corner of the mouth being forced into a pretend smile position.

It seemed to me that they hardly ever spent time in the same room. I knew this was not good because when I didn't want to be in the same room as my little sister it wasn't for a good reason: I didn't want to be near her.

Then the arguments started, which was a shock to me as I had no recollection of them ever raising their voices to each other. But this was when I knew their time was over and I would be a kid with divorced parents.

I cannot imagine any child wanting their parents to separate but there I was, fourteen years old having suffered nine years of bullying and my parents were getting divorced.

My view of the world had been well and truly programmed into my young, impressionable mind. I was feeling lost, scared and alone but more than anything I was angry.

I was fourteen years old with all my beliefs around family, myself and other people firmly imprinted into my young mind. This set of experiences would forge who I would be for years to come, never did I feel I had any choice or control over it.

The power of our initial years on the planet can guide

you for the rest of your life, whether it is positive or negative.

Tip for everyday-

The secret to becoming the boss of your own life is believing you can. It is understanding the fact that you can gain control of your life once you become an adult.

To start to take back control you must recognise the parts of your life you want to change, what worked for you growing up does not necessarily work for you now.

Everyone has the right to create their own story, whatever the chapters before this moment in time have told you. It can be exciting, scary and full of anxiety. But I am asking you to start believing in yourself, be the J.K. Rowling of your own story and start to create something magical.

Task-

In the last chapter we looked at how your life is impacted negatively by your critical voice. Continue to grow that awareness by listing your negative thought and behaviour patterns, what do you do regularly that makes you feel shit?

Pick a single negative part of your life and find out as much as you can about this single topic. Ask questions. Where did it come from? What benefits have you received from having this belief? How does it impact you negatively now? Is there anywhere in the process you could make a change? How do you want to be now? Why would you keep it in place? What are your barriers to changing? Get to know the topic honestly and then follow that with conscious action.

Don't overload yourself by trying to change everything you find in one go. Slow and steady wins the race. Above all, believe that you have a choice over how the rest of your story is written.

Further reading-

Look at the book *They F@#k You Up* by Oliver James, he talks openly about the impact on our futures based on the experiences we have in our early years.

Universal Lesson #4

You get from life what you are willing to put

into it.

When you take a leap of faith to live a life that you desire, you must invest in it whole-heartedly. It's true: you get out of life what you put into it. The universe will support you if you devote your beliefs to what you want and act on those beliefs.

It will take bravery on your part but the universe will pay you back for your bravery by helping you create the self you want.

The moments in life where you do not feel brave at all but you still go ahead and do that one thing you have been talking yourself out of are bloody inspiring, empowering and life affirming.

You got this.

I want to take you back to the jungle in Nepal, where I was investing fuck all into my journey towards being a superhero.

I had made no effort to dispel what I assumed must be my new family's first impression of me. If anything, my mind had used that as an excuse to reinforce all the negative thoughts I had about myself.

The first seven days were a culture shock; I was not expecting it to be as tough as I was experiencing.

There were a few things I found hard: the heat, the diet, impossible communication and the lack of confidence in me from the family I was staying with.

To be fair to the family, I had not really given them much evidence that I was capable, especially as I was using every opportunity to not embrace where I was. On the second day of being there I asked if I could go with them to the fields to work but was told probably best I stay at the home, which left me visibly pissed off, but secretly underneath relieved. It was hot and I was tired, oh and bloody lazy.

The fat jibe whilst having my first shower had really got its claws into my psyche, then I got told by a highly informative young kid that 'moto' means fat in Nepalese. I felt like screaming at the idiots. I remember thinking I was ready to go, I wanted to pack my bags and leave. But instead, I fell into my autopilot thinking and confirmed all they were saying at every opportunity. I began calling myself the fat Englishman to anyone that would listen.

It is bloody hard work investing in a journey you know nothing about. I was so far out of my comfort zone my poor little brain did not have a fucking clue what was going on.

The first time I tasted Dal Bhat, the rice and lentil curry/soup with some chopped vegetables in it, I was impressed with how they could make it with very few utensils, in just a small clay oven in their home.

By day three I was full to the brim with it and telling myself I would never eat rice again in my life. We were having it three to four times a day: the exact same meal for breakfast, lunch and dinner. I could not work out how the whole family ate every meal as if they had never eaten it before, the joy on their faces as they scooped piles of rice into their mouths with their hands. I did try eating with my hands. Let me tell you, rice straight off the heat burns. They didn't even flinch; they must have had asbestos skin.

I spent seven days wallowing in my own self-pity, directing my anger at everyone else and their stupid decisions to not let me do anything. I spent my days picking corn apart, watching everyone else going off to do the hard graft of picking and maintaining the fields and being an essential cog in the workings of the home.

I was exhausted physically and mentally; the heat and the environment had taken it out of me and I had not even done anything.

Luckily for me there was a Canadian lady, Gloria, staying in the home next to ours, she was my age and was doing the same thing as me. She had packed it all up and decided she wanted an adventure; she was staying with the brother of the main man I was staying with.

I really wanted to talk to Gloria about my experience so far, but I was so wrapped up in my own shit and insecurities that my ego was not letting me show any sign of weakness.

I had to change something and I had to do it quick. Time was disappearing around me and my adventure was turning into a personal nightmare. Here I was at the start of an amazing experience sulking because my ego had been dented. I was having a childish tantrum because I was not getting my own way. What an idiot! This was then provoking my subconscious to reignite my insecurities about my weight.

I pulled Gloria aside one day. 'Can we have a chat about this whole experience we are having?' I gingerly asked.

'Of course, what's up?' she said with her usual smiling face.

Well, that was enough for me to open the floodgates. 'I fucking hate it here. I'm not enjoying any part of it. They won't let me do anything. I'm knackered and I don't think this is for me.'

There was a visible look of shock on her face. 'I am glad it is not just me.'

The sense of relief I felt in that moment was immense. 'What do you mean? Have you been finding it hard too? You always seem to be smiling and doing things.'

She then imparted her wise words of wisdom. 'I figured that I can be struggling and not feel comfortable, but it is what it is. So, if I can't change it, I'm just going to get on with it.'

Kapow! That was like being hit around the face with a wet fish, waking me up from a seven-day slumber. I told Gloria how much that resonated with me. 'Maybe I need to take control of what I can, which means myself.'

'Well, we don't have any control over anybody else,' she replied, re-teaching me a lesson I had been teaching my clients for years.

Gloria had been on her heroes' journey for about nine months, so was a lot further along the path of self-discovery than I was. I had been nurturing and indulging negativities instead of focusing on the positives that were occurring every day right in front of me'.

'Mark, I believe you're a warrior. You've stepped away from the normality of life to walk a new path. To face unknown barriers and questions that cannot be answered, all for the desire of a more fulfilled life. How can that not be something to be proud of?' What a powerful statement that was from Gloria, she really helped me look at myself through different eyes.

I must tell you, that made me feel emotional, the understanding this stranger was showing me was overwhelming.

'Thank you', I mumbled through quivering lips, trying to hide the feelings that were building up in me.

I didn't want to keep feeling guilty and doubtful about the risk I had taken, I wanted to learn and grow, that was the whole reason for coming.

I wanted to be the brave warrior Gloria described me as.

What a difference a day can make. I was going to be brave and bloody invest in this risk I had taken, no matter where it took me.

I got up early the next day and offered to help whisk the curd that gets done every morning before breakfast. There was a large earthenware pot with a large pole stuck in it, like a giant whisk, this was tied to one of the posts inside the kitchen area with a frayed piece of string. I sat down on the clay floor with my bare feet supporting the pot, then with another piece of string wrapped around the pole I started to row. It was kind of like when you start a fire using a friction bow. Back and forth, my arms were aching, my arse was going numb from sitting on the floor; I had sweat dripping into my eyes, but I also had a smile going from ear to ear. This was so much fun, why hadn't I done this before? An hour later we had curd; I was so excited.

I did some digging around the home and broke the spade, but they just smiled and laughed when I tried to explain what had happened.

I said to the father, 'I want to go and work the fields with you today.' You could see the trepidation on his face, but I was not to be held back anymore.

'I am not sure good idea, extremely hot, hard work,' he explained, seemingly trying his best to be diplomatic.

I was not to be deterred, so I grabbed a giant weaved basket and headed to the corn fields with the family. If you have never picked corn before it is not as easy as it is made to look. I had hands full of small cuts and my T-shirt was stuck to my back like cling film wrapped around a hot sausage roll.

I worked for hours in the heat and smiled the whole time.

I had taken control of my own involvement. I had realised that my time here so far had been spent moaning about not being allowed to do things, but never being brave enough to put myself forward with any gusto to get involved.

The day I spent in the field with them stripping corn, cutting back unwanted foliage and packing giant wicker baskets was an eye opener. The baskets were heavy when full and I was put to shame by the women who just casually heaved them onto their backs, whilst I looked like a turtle with a block of flats on his back instead of a shell. I was starting to learn that I would only get from my adventure what I was willing to put in, whether that makes me uncomfortable or not.

I started to notice things that I had missed previously:

the kids would get up at six in the morning to walk one-and-a-half hours up hill to school. They would return in the afternoon, have some Dal Baht, then go and work on their crops all with a zest for life that I had never experienced. They had nothing compared to where I came from, but in fact had everything. The kids would entertain themselves with a battered old bicycle wheel and a stick, the children laughed uncontrollably while I was swinging them around in the air, I could pick fruit an arm's length from where I was staying, the bond of a family that worked together like clockwork, the care they showed complete strangers and the level of hard work to survive as a family.

I consciously fought my critical mind that was trying to make me feel guilty for not noticing before, but as Gloria said, 'it is what it is.' I couldn't go back in time, so wanted to keep moving forward.

Gloria had told me about an outcrop about twenty minutes' walk away from the home, which was a place where the goat herders went to have a rest up whilst transporting

their goats around. I decided it was somewhere I needed to

see.

'I'm going for a walk on my own,' I explained to the

head of the house with my biggest smile.

'No, not on your own, not safe.'

I was determined. 'I'll be OK, I promise, I will take care.

I'll see you in a few hours.' I didn't really leave him any room

for argument.

I made it there without any catastrophes. I did not fall

into a rice field and drown, I did not get eaten by a rogue

snake, I didn't even get lost on my first solo outing,

miraculous or what?

The outcrop was a small, raised, grassy platform

surrounded by a crumbling brick wall. There was a large tree

that offered shade to the weary herders, giving them some

small respite from the day's heat.

You could see for miles: there was the river winding through the hills like a giant serpent, the hills were so green, vibrant with life. You could see rice field after rice field hanging on to the sides of the hills, with the occasional dwelling scattered in the wildness of it all.

There I was sat on an outcrop halfway up a mountain in Nepal, sweat pouring off my ears as my bandana failed miserably at containing my non-stop head leakage. A bandana, I hear you say, for the love of God man you are forty years old. Trust me, four weeks before I left England the idea would have made me cringe, but I knew I was coming to Nepal and I knew I was going to sweat like no man before me. So, I thought I would roll back the years, grab some lost confidence in how I look and buy some colourful bandanas. The one I wore in that moment was bright red and made me stick out like an English post box in the middle of the jungle.

A big red head walking around amongst the green of the jungle, like a beacon for every creature and bug for miles around. I am sure the locals praised the day I turned up, as it would give them a break from being bitten and I would take over the mantle as the mosquito god of Harkapur.

It honestly felt like someone had sat me next to an open fire for the first two weeks and I had not been unable to gain any relief from a heat that seemed to get into every pore of my body.

So far, I had woken up each morning feeling exhausted from lack of sleep and my clothes wet from the furnace I called a bedroom. Then I got up and remembered that the bedroom was the coolest place I would be that day and when I walked out of the door I would be hit by a blanket of suffocating humidity. It was unlike anything I had experienced in my life; it certainly had no resemblance to the mild summers and even milder winters we have in good old Blighty.

As I sat on my newly found outcrop in the mountains looking down the valley to the town of Trishuli, my thoughts began to find some clarity and excitement.

I started to realise their way of life had humbled me over the first two weeks and had left me feeling guilty for not appreciating it. They had taught me so much about enjoying the small things and not living life wanting for more. The happiness in the small family shined like the brightest star, pulling everyone close to them into their orbit of simple joy.

I had not consciously taken any notice until today, but one day the week before the father had walked uphill for four hours to buy a large bag of potatoes, then walked back home with it over his shoulders. He had swapped some of his crop. What an inspiring way to provide for your family. Not only did he do this but on his return, he ate a plate of rice then went to work in his own fields for another four hours before heading home with a basket half his size slung over his shoulder full of corn.

How had I not noticed this at the time? They were teaching me so much without them even realising it.

As I sat on the outcrop that day trying to calm my emotions and reflect on the start of what had been an epic journey, a sense that something had led me to that point washed over me. There was a reason for me making the choices that had brought me there. It is hard to explain, it was like déjà vu, as if I had been sat on that outcrop previously, as if it was part of my destiny to be sat there exactly in that moment.

The beautiful outcrop was to become a sacred place of simplicity for me over my last week or so. It was more than just a quiet space for me to think; it was somewhere I was accepted, by myself and strangers walking by.

I was making connections: this tiny little outcrop tucked away in the hills of Nepal was changing me. I would visit it on my own a few times over the next few days, each time feeling like we were building a strong bond between us.

I sat or lay there in silent meditation, drinking in the positive effect it was having on me. My thoughts were becoming clearer: I would have the wind gently caressing my face, cooling me down so I could think clearly. The outcrop was allowing me to be there, nowhere else. My anxieties had no place there, my fears had gently drifted into the background.

It taught me to stop looking for more; what I had right in front of me was plenty to keep me happy if I noticed it.

I started to think perhaps this is what Gloria's description of us being warriors meant, the idea of being a warrior within my own life started to excite me.

My new outlook on this experience was enabling me to think clearer and my next step became crystal clear one day whilst sitting on my idyllic outcrop under the tree that allowed some shade from the heat.

This six weeks in Nepal would not be the end to this adventure: I wanted to experience more. The sense of being completely out of my comfort zone was energising and life confirming, even if very, very scary and I wanted more of it.

I knew when I returned home, I was going risk it all for a path I now knew I was meant to take. This new belief literally flowed through my very cells. I had complete trust in my instinct and it was telling me that I should see more of the world, be in situations that scared me, be the superhero of my own future and become all that I was meant to be.

The three weeks at the home stay had been a roller coaster of a ride. I'm not sure what I was expecting when I made the decision to go there, but I'm pretty sure I wasn't expecting this level of self-discovery.

The experience had allowed me to discover myself without all the safety blankets that being at home provided, which turned out to be scarier than I had imagined when sitting in the comfort of my own home deciding to go to Nepal for six weeks.

At times I felt vulnerable to the world and my own thoughts. It taught me very quickly that I was not as confident as I let on most of the time, but that this was OK.

The last few days were brilliant; I felt alive. On the last night we chatted, we laughed and sang the night away and I went to bed with a sense of joy in my heart.

The return bus ride to Kathmandu was a sign of how much I had changed in the three weeks I had spent in the jungle. I managed to get another psychopath for a bus driver but this time had no fears of falling off the side of a mountain.

Again, I was surrounded by Nepalese men and women coughing their lungs up. I thought the guy in front of me was going to die he was coughing non-stop for the whole time but he lived, thankfully.

My new-found ability to embrace the journey rather than fear, it allowed me to notice just how beautiful this country was, full of steep mountain hills, gushing rivers, and a huge variety of vibrant colours. I was getting lost in my surroundings.

This was until a battered old black Mercedes came around a blind corner on our side of the road, causing my crazy driver to slam the brakes on and swerve out of his way.

I sat in my chair shaking my head mouthing fucking idiots. As soon as I had, the Mercedes braked to a halt. At this point four of the biggest Nepalese blokes I had ever seen jumped out of their car, all wearing white vest tops and covered in tattoos, looking very pissed off. I did not realise Nepal had a mafia but these guys were certainly acting as if they were it.

At this point my head was thinking, *oh bollocks they saw me.* They had got out to drag the only white guy off the bus and give him a kicking for having the front to point out how crap their driving was.

As it turned out the bus driver must have had the same reaction as me, because one of them came to his window and started shouting at him, trying to get him out of the bus. Sensibly the bus driver refused to get out, so the biggest guy in the group reached through his window and punched him a few times around the face. There was then a few more shouted words and they returned to their car, leaving my not-so-psycho bus driver looking very uneasy.

But there I was as happy as pig in shit. I had gone from detesting being in Nepal to absolutely loving it with every ounce of my being. I felt indestructible the rest of the journey; I knew that to fully invest in a new journey, I must fully invest in the idea that it will not all be smooth sailing. I was excited and pumped to find out what was next.

Bravery comes in so many forms. You have been brave to start reading this book. It takes bravery to put yourself at the top of your importance list and even more to then act on it.

I do not believe bravery is about always getting it right. It's about trying to make positive changes in your life. It's about that conscious investment in yourself, about growing a belief and taking responsibility for your own actions and thoughts.

Everyone has a brave warrior inside screaming to be

set free. Be brave, let them out and watch your world change.

Tip for everyday-

Investing in a leap of faith is not as easy as it sounds because your old beliefs will always try and pull you back to your old way of seeing yourself and the world around you.

But if you have been putting in place the lessons from previous chapters you will be starting to build a conscious awareness of your world. This is your foundation for change.

You are starting to become conscious of your own life; that takes bravery and commitment. It's no small feat so you should be proud of yourself.

If you want parts of your life to change, only you can make them changes. Be brave, take a risk on you, it will be worth it, I promise.

Task-

Have a look at your life. Are there any areas where you can take full responsibility? Are there areas in your life that you always hear yourself say 'They make me do this,' 'It's their fault I feel this way.' If there are, sit in that experience and take personal responsibility for it being different.

When we use sentences like the above ones, we hand over all our power to that person. Take it back, it's yours to keep. Look at the role you take within these situations and instead of putting the responsibility onto others, look at what you can change.

Use your journal for this, give yourself a visual reminder of what you are learning, the new processes you are creating and reflect on what you write.

Further reading-

There is a Buddhist monk named Thich Nhat Hanh, he speaks openly about the power we have inside of us. Check out *Fear: Essential wisdom for getting through the storm,* where he talks about fear and how to work with it so you can approach life with confidence.

Universal Lesson #5

Fighting against the fear only makes it

stronger.

As humans we evolved the fight or flight response when we were cave people, this is the reaction we feel when faced with a harmful event, attack or threat to our survival. It is a chemical response that prepares our bodies to either stay in the situation or run away from the threat.

Trying to get rid of the fear or anxiety will only make it grow; they are both there for a particularly good reason. We were given the fight-or-flight response to protect us, to keep us away from roaming dinosaurs and other cave people. It is important for us to have a certain level of stress and anxiety within us but not so much that we allow it to direct our choices.

Anxiety takes away the belief that we have a choice in a certain situation but you always have a plethora of choices, even if your history is telling you that you don't.

It was the 17th of January 2014 and I had reached Bangkok airport; I had walked away from everything I knew. I had given up my counselling practice, handed the keys back to the house I rented, sold my old banger of a motor, and put every penny I had into one bank account. My whole life for the foreseeable future was in the rucksack on my back.

I had stepped off the plane with butterflies in my stomach from the uncertainty of what lay ahead, I was tired, aching all over and overwhelmed with the enormity of what I had chosen to do. But I felt free for the first time ever in my life. Free from the expectations of the world around me.

I had the hostel address in my hand and I decided to try and find it by using public transport, my tiny little bit of research had told me you could get their equivalent to the underground into the centre of Bangkok.

Then I walked out the front doors of the airport and was hit in the face by the extreme heat which felt like I had just dived headfirst into an incinerator. Along with this, came an overwhelming belief that I had lost all my intelligence and common sense and if I attempted this feat of reaching the hostel, I would end up lost in one of the craziest cities in the world, so I bottled it.

With that I grabbed a taxi. Unfortunately, the driver knew as much English as I did Thai. Even after showing him the address on paper, he looked none the wiser but he pulled away and started heading towards the city. He was on the phone as he was driving; I presume trying to find out where the bloody hell we were going. Bangkok is made up of mini districts and I knew mine was on the outskirts but other than that I was clueless, so I put my complete faith in this stranger.

A couple of hours later, we found it tucked away on a back street. Once you get into the internal workings of

Bangkok you realise how much of a maze it is. I remember sitting in the back of the cab thinking how the hell am I going to work this out? I would have to just sit in the hostel for the first week and not risk leaving it in case I couldn't find it again and ended up like a modern-day Alice in Wonderland wondering around a landscape that didn't make any sense.

As I stood in front of the hostel door, I took a moment and a few deep breaths. I was uncomfortable in my clothes; sweat had become the prominent smell and my T-shirt looked like I had been swimming in it.

I gingerly opened the door and walked into a room of strange faces, time seemed to stop for an instant as they all looked up and judged this new person entering their midst. Then the smiles came, people got up and introduced themselves, people shook my hand, gave me hugs and there was lots of welcoming name introductions.

I was full of relief. Part of me expected them to stand up and point at me saying, what the fuck are you doing here old man?

The room was amazing, there was a mix of ages from eighteen to fifties. As I sat down to introduce myself to this new group of strangers, I felt myself relaxing with the knowledge I wasn't the oldest or the biggest.

I ended up spending about an hour with this group before I got shown to my dormitory. In this time, I had a captive audience who were genuinely impressed and interested in what had brought me here.

The fear of being judged started to dwindle; these complete strangers had done more for my confidence levels than anything had over the recent months of preparation. It felt as if they all knew about my anxieties and fears for my journey, which I am sure they all did as they had all started travelling at some point.

I was so tired I slept like a teenager that night. (I have never understood the saying *slept like a baby*. What you mean you woke up every two hours after shitting yourself and needing to be fed? Doesn't sound like a great night's sleep to me!)

The next five days were a bit of a blur but there were a few things that stood out.

I am fairly sure the Buddha would be disgusted at the visible signs of prosperity that people attach to him in Bangkok such as the huge gold statues that could feed a thousand people if melted down. After a walk around the big temples in Bangkok, I was left feeling uncomfortable as if it were all very false, using the Buddha as a way of promoting tourism and wealth rather than simple inner happiness.

I went on a tour around one of the bigger temples to try and get an insight into the history.

The guide turned to me and pointed at my ear. 'You have great ears," he said. "You will live to be over one hundred years old!'

Normally I would not take any notice, but I quite liked the idea of this. 'Thank you that's good to know,' I replied. I'm sure if he had told me I was going to die by the time I was fifty I would have said it was all a load of bollocks.

I found myself hunting out greenery whilst I was in Bangkok. It was as if all the buildings, traffic and people were sucking the energy away from me. By the end of the week, it felt like all these man-made buildings where keeping me trapped in a place I did not want to be. It was like I was having my life sucked out of my veins by an invisible force.

Even though I felt lost and intimidated by it all, I felt complete faith in the fact I was where I was meant to be. I was not comfortable in the heat, with the language barrier or not having a clue how to get around but it did not matter.

The last day in Bangkok I decided to wash all my clothes so I could start afresh on the next part of my journey. I took some washing down to a street launderette that had been recommended by one of the blokes in the hostel.

I came across two drunk old ladies sitting out by their machines. I tried to explain what I wanted but no one understood a word that was being said, and one old girl was very friendly with her hands (if you know what I mean). I felt so uncomfortable with the language barrier, physical contact, people watching as they walked by laughing and me being centre of attention. So I left my washing and they told me to come back in fifty minutes and I ran away from there as quick as I could.

When I got back to the hostel, I had a strange feeling of disappointment in myself. I was annoyed that I had not allowed myself to relax, as I was sure that these ladies just wanted to have a laugh and were being friendly. I had been intimidated by the whole situation; I was not feeling brave at all. I stood there in the hostel criticising myself for letting my fear of being made to look stupid in public make me run away like a scared child, when I should have had the balls to stay in the anxiety ridden situation. I told myself that I would try and become more aware in these situations and try not to embrace my fight or flight response quite so easily.

When I went to pick up my washing twenty minutes after the time the old girls had given me, it was still in the washer, so they told me to sit down.

Shit, I thought, I had not been expecting to have to put my new attitude to the test quite so soon. Anyway, I sat down and we spent the next twenty minutes drinking their alcohol (Hong Thang, which is a Thai whiskey). It was like drinking fire, no wonder they were pissed. They offered me some of their lunch while I waited, which was just as hot as the alcohol.

There were lots of rubbing of thighs (them rubbing mine, not the other way round) and lots of laughter at no one understanding a damn thing the other was saying. Honestly, these two old birds had the complexions of E.T but they were full of life enjoying every moment and you could tell by their cheeky grins they knew exactly what they were doing. It was bloody hilarious.

You may well have guessed also that the bloke in the

hostel had stitched me up and knew exactly what I was walking into, so thanks to him for the lesson, wanker.

The experiences of Bangkok left me wanting more and as I left the next day, I knew I would not be walking away from situations that scared me. They are the ones where you forge the stories that highlight your new journey.

It is not a smooth ride taking this path, as this story points out. The process of being brave enough to step outside the box is full of steps forward and then steps back. You will have moments when you are not feeling brave; you will want to go back to your safe, understood lifestyle.

Being brave and stepping out of my comfort zone created the perfect situation for fear and anxiety to breed, as I had taken all the certainty of my future away. This was a perceived certainty, as no one knows the future. But based on my history, my mind had created my future and it was desperate to pull me back to my comfortable, unchallenging lifestyle. Yours will try too; don't let it.

Tip for everyday-

The best way to lessen the fear is to not avoid situations that you are fearful of or that make you uncomfortable, as the more you avoid the bigger the fear gets. It isn't about not feeling uncomfortable, it's about becoming present with the feelings.

Anxiety breeds the more we feed it, so if you can be totally conscious in any of the fearful moments you choose to be in, it enables you to take the control back.

As you work your way through this book, please don't think you will go straight through without the need to return to previous lessons, this is unrealistic and can create unnecessary pressure.

Even though I have reached the end of this particular journey, I spend a lot of time going back to these lessons and must re-teach myself the ones I am not keeping in place.

Task-

I want you to think of one thing that scares you. Write it in your journal then formulate a way you can face it. Can someone support you? Can you figure out where this fear comes from? Is it yours or has someone passed it onto you? Then face it down, step out of your box and be brave, look the fear in the eyes and do it. Then journal it, be open and honest about the experience.

Always remember, feeling fear when you are facing fear is normal. Don't beat yourself up if you are scared of facing a fear: you are supposed to be.

Further reading-

Please take time to read the book *Feel The Fear & Do It Anyway* by Dr Susan Jeffers; it's a great book offering help and advice around not letting the fear rule your life.

Universal Lesson #6

Learning how to ground yourself to the Earth will bring you control over overwhelming situations.

We live a huge part of our lives on autopilot, our fears and anxieties being driven by our past and our fears for the future. This autopilot living can leave us feeling like we have no control over our lives, that we will always be led by our subconscious programming.

Grounding is when you consciously make the decision to connect to something positive when your thoughts and the world around you seem overwhelming. Grounding focusses the mind, helps bring clarity of thought and brings control back into your hands.

The planet we live on gives us a huge number of possibilities for this; it surrounds us with beauty and miraculous things every day.

Finding your anchors, the thing or things that make you smile, relaxing and reconnecting, no matter what the situation, is what grounding is all about. Look around, the universe has put lots in front of us, we might as well take advantage of it.

Finding your grounding anchors is all part of the adventure, so approach it as such. Everything you try is another experience, another lesson to be learnt. Put in place what you have learnt in previous chapters and go out into the world to search, like Indiana Jones searching for the crystal skulls.

The first few chapters of this book should have helped you become aware of some possible changes you can make in your world but I know, from my own experience and helping others, that this is a daunting prospect at times. The ability to ground yourself in moments of doubt is extremely powerful so having the tool of grounding in your locker will enable you to continually move forward.

In 2011 my Mum asked me to do something on her bucket list with her. She wanted to go to Peru and see Machu Pichu on her birthday. How could I refuse? Well, I could not and did not, so an adventure with my Mum it would be.

It was an awe-inspiring trip. We saw Condors at Colca Canyon, ambled around Cusco, drove to the highest drivable point in Peru, bathed in natural warm springs looking over the mountains, had a few scary bus and plane rides and I even tried their national dish of Guinea pig (although I was still really hungry afterwards as you would need about ten to fill you up.)

We got on amazingly well and I was taken aback by my Mum's eagerness to give everything a try, this coming from a lady who is scared by lots of things, including flying and heights.

I think putting aside your fears to do something you love is a real sign of strength and my admiration for my Mum grew by the day. We also had lots of laughs along the way.

The highlight of the trip was the couple of days we spent at Machu Pichu, where Mum had booked a hotel at the side of the river Urubamba

We got to Aguas Calientes, the little town at the bottom of Machu Picchu by train, which was an amazing ride bending through the mountains and scenery you could die for. As soon as we got off the train, we were surrounded by steep hills covered in green jungle, flowers of all colours hit your senses and the sound of roaring water from the river gave me a sense of being alive.

I found myself mesmerized by the river from the first moment I saw it, I felt I needed to find time to be nearer it, feel it, get to know it. It didn't make much sense to me at the time but all I could focus on was the mysterious river that was generating feelings I had not felt before. Even the name,

Urubamba, had a magical feel to it – like a kind of tribal dance to call on the gods.

But we had plans so it had to wait. As we wandered around the town at the bottom of the mountains, my mind kept being drawn back to the river.

We woke early the next day exhilarated about the adventure ahead, although my Mum was nervous of the bus ride up as she knew the little roads would be cradling the side of a mountain. This was not helped by us getting a flat tyre halfway up, all we heard was the bus thudding suddenly and not riding as smooth as it had previously. The driver got out and searched the bus for the issue then the news that we had a flat tyre worked its way to where we were sitting. The driver then decided to drive the rest of the way with said flat tyre; as you can imagine this calmed my Mum's nerves right down, if only!

But we did make it to the top with a few gasps and seat clenching, to be welcomed by dozens of other buses and enthusiastic visitors all trying to get a glimpse of this amazing landscape.

This is the issue with beautiful places around the world: everyone and his sister want to see them. I would love to find places on this planet that no one knows of so I can just sit there, on my own, without all the furore that surrounds a tourist attraction. But there we were, part of the masses.

It turned out that this year was the one-hundred-year anniversary of the site being found, so we got a special stamp in our passports.

If you have never been to Machu Picchu, it is hard to explain the impact it has on you when you first walk around the corner and see it spread out in front of you. The best word that springs to mind is awe. My jaw dropped at the spectacular view bombarding my eyes; it was breath-taking.

We spent some time on our own just wandering around the ruins. It was the most serene, emotive place I had ever been. You could feel history seeping into your veins, connecting you to a time that was hard to comprehend. Over recent years I had become a firm believer in energies and how it connects us to everything around us Whilst sitting there I could feel the energy of the people that had lived there.

We experienced something special that day: mother and son having a truly awesome adventure and on my Mum's birthday too. Neither of us wanted to leave but our time was up, so begrudgingly we left for the bus ride back down the mountain. It was less eventful on the way back which was a nice thing for everyone concerned.

We walked along the river on our way back to the hotel and I made the decision that I would get up early in the morning and go out on my own. I still could not shift the sense that I had more to learn from this river.

When we got back, I snuck off to reception to ask if they could bring out a cake with a candle on it during our meal. Took some interpretation skills from the receptionist but we got there in the end; when they brought it out and the whole restaurant sang happy birthday - my mum's face was an absolute picture.

I set my alarm for six o'clock the next morning. It came around quick as my night's sleep had been erratic due to me thinking about the river Urubamba. I was feeling pumped and electrified, as if I were going to meet a Guru who would give me all the answers to life's questions.

As I walked outside the hotel the river was straight in front of me, its roaring sound beckoning me to come closer. I walked a little bit out of the town as I wanted my time by the river to be as free of people as possible, until I came across a possible way down to its riverbanks.

If my Mum had been with me, she would have been terrified as I scrambled down the embankment next to the river. I wanted to be close to it, close enough to touch its rampaging power. After a few slips and heart stopping moments, I made it to the giant rocks that were strategically placed around the side of the river. At this point I became aware that it had been a risky move climbing down: one slip and the raging river would have swallowed me up and spat me out miles downriver without a second thought.

The first thing that got me was the noise. It was so loud when up close and personal but it had a rhythmic sound to it that was mesmerizing. I remember standing there thinking that I needed to take as many pictures as possible, which I did for the first ten minutes. Then it hit me like a wave: what was I doing? I was missing this moment because I wanted to prove I had been there to others. I realized this wasn't about anyone else, this was just for me so I put the camera in my little rucksack.

It's easy to forget we always have the best camera available to us: our memory.

I spent the next two hours sat on my rock: meditating, listening, smelling, touching (not myself) and taking it all in. The surroundings were divine, a huge variety of plants, colours that bombarded your vision, a smell that was so clean and pure that you felt more alive every time you took a breath in. But I was always drawn back to the river as if it were trying to get my attention; I had never in my life felt this calm. Even though I knew one slip off my rock would mean my demise; the river would show no mercy towards me if I was not respectful.

As I sat there the river's personality started to take form. To recognise it, I was using a part of my brain that had seemed dormant up until that point. My imagination was starting to run wild, my view of the world changing, my connection to the world around me taking a new form. I felt as if I was part of it instead of a separate entity living within it.

Spiritual journeys are always full of doubt, normally led by a past that is trying to keep you in your comfort zone.

But at that moment, in time the river was connecting its personality to mine, it was reminding me that I am strong when needed but gentle at the core, that barriers will be put in front of me but I would always find a way to continue my journey. There would be times of calmness and times of turmoil but I would be in control of them, I would protect and provide for the people I love. I would be determined to follow my own quest, I would be honest and true to myself and I would always stay connected to who I truly am. I was so conscious for those two hours that any fears or anxieties did not exist, I had found something that grounded me to the earth. That I knew could calm me if the world seemed too much.

I found it hard to walk away from the river, as I felt we had bonded, that it had shown me that water was one of my anchors to the moment. I knew that if I had any doubts in the future, I just needed to find some water and reconnect, that this would bring me confidence.

When I returned home, I found myself reminiscing over the river Urubamba, wanting to be back there, to feel that connection again. It was fucking annoying that I did not have a cascading river at the end of my garden. I started to lose the connection because I became obsessed with the idea that to connect to water, the water itself had to be on the same scale as it was in Peru.

It took me a while before I started to learn the lessons that I have explained in the first few chapters but once I did the connection flowed back. I could then consciously quieten my critical voice; I could consciously step back from the situation and put my grounding skills in place.

This has led to water being a huge guiding light for me when times are tough, it has given me so much strength and control over the years.

I have always hunted out water wherever I have been in the world but the biggest trick is to find it on your own doorstep. With practice, I can now ground myself in the shower, stirring a cup of tea or listening to the gentle flow of a small stream.

If all this is not possible, then use your memories to

recreate it in your mind. Our mind's eye can create anything if we nurture it kindly. If I cannot find water, I will close my eyes and take a seat next to a stream in a wood or next to a cascading river or beneath a glistening waterfall.

Finding a place of calm and inner tranquility when the world around you is overwhelming will give you a solid foundation that will enable anything to grow.

Tip for everyday-

We live on a planet that is full of grounding opportunities but to find them you must get conscious.

Becoming more conscious of your life is a huge change; it is this fear of change that will fight against you putting grounding skills in place. This is because your autopilot feels all it makes you do now is what is best for you, so you trying to tell it there are new, positive ways for you to deal with situations will make it fight for normality.

A great way of connecting to the things that help ground you is to use your senses; you can't be anywhere else with your thoughts if you are one hundred percent concentrating on using a sense.

Task-

Every Monday morning, I want you to pick one of your senses then during every day of that week use that sense to notice something new. Smell the leaves on the floor, close your eyes and taste your dinner slowly, look at yourself in the mirror and notice all the wonderful story telling signs on your face, close your eyes and hold an object in your hands, close your eyes and listen to a piece of music, watch the movement of the clouds, feel the wind on your bare skin.

What makes you smile? What makes you laugh? What makes you feel calm? What makes you feel energised? These are the questions you need to ask yourself. If nothing comes forward, don't panic. This is an opportunity for you to go on an adventure, to try new things in the search for what grounds you when it's all going bat shit crazy.

Oh, and don't forget, put all this new experience in your wonderfully evolving journal.

Further reading- There is a magical little book called *Who Moved My Cheese?* by Spencer Johnson, it cleverly takes you through the process of change. The inner battles we come across and the power of accepting change in your life, you will not regret reading this gem.

Universal Lesson #7

Your past does not have to dictate your future.

Our negative experiences and the resulting demons that get implanted, provide a huge opportunity for development. But it's hard to learn the lessons the universe is trying to teach you when you feel shoulder deep in the shit.

By now you will have learnt some things about yourself by reading this book, some good, some seemingly not so good.

This chapter is about helping you to see no matter what has happened in your past, your present can be anything you decide it to be. If you saw yourself a certain way previously, you can see yourself differently now.

Know that the journey to find the real YOU will be

full of moments you would rather wipe from your memory. But you can't. There are no magical Harry Potter wands here: we just need to learn that our pasts do not have to dictate our present or future.

In 1987 I was fourteen years old. I was stood in the tuck queue at school waiting patiently for my Wham bar and packet of crisps.

My regular bully that had followed me from primary school came along and pushed me out of the queue and as a good obedient kid I put my head down and walked to the back of the queue. As I reached the back, I heard the teacher running the tuck shop shout out, "Woody, don't let him push you out, you were there first."

I gingerly replied, 'It's OK sir, I don't mind.'

'Woody it's your place. You stand there.'

Of course, by now all the students were watching with excitement at the scene unfolding in front of them, including all the bully's mates who were the tough group a couple of years older than me.

I was terrified but I felt I couldn't just stand there, so I walked back to my original spot and told the lad it was my space and he needed to get to the back of the line. I was shaking from head to toe, thinking to myself *what the fucking hell are you doing?*

He went to push me away and this is when it all changed. Something happened to me in that moment. I just looked at him and shook my head, silently telling him his time was over.

There was a heat running through my veins, as if all the years of hidden fear, sadness and insecurity had turned into an unbreakable force within every molecule of my body. My eyes felt like they had burning fires in them, then the lad that had bullied me on and off for eight years turned around and went to the back of the line without saying a word.

If it had not been for the teacher telling me to stick up

100

for myself, I'm not sure where I would be now, probably living a completely different life. But he did and instantly, in that moment, a new young man was born.

Fuck me I felt amazing, like a superhero who has just found his superpowers. People next to me in the queue were tapping me on the shoulder saying well done, the bully's mates did nothing to stick up for their friend. I was untouchable, invincible, and strong. Shit did I feel strong.

The above incident coincided with my parents' separation, which gave me the belief that I had to step up and look after my Mum and little sister. To be able to do this at home, I had to become someone else away from it.

The last two years of school I had no interest in. I went from being an exceptionally good student to a student who was just there so I could see my mates and girls. I started to re-invent myself, using my newfound confidence and sense of invincibility as the foundation to build a new personality. It was a completely new view of myself and the world around me; nothing intimidated me.

This was apparent the day another student pulled a butterfly knife at me because I had been pushing him for a scrap. I just nonchalantly said to him, 'Try and stab me then, see what happens.' The look of worry on his face that I was willing to get stabbed just to prove myself, made him put the knife away and walk away silently.

I became a young man who needed to be seen a certain way. I was a yob; someone you couldn't mess with.

I would go up town at fifteen or sixteen years old and get pissed, smoke and fight. Luckily my Mum was quite naive, so with a gargle of Insignia aftershave and rubbing dirt into my hands, I could hide the smell of cigarette smoke and alcohol enough for her not to notice.

My best mate, Ant, and I would decide who would start the fight that night, so before we left the house, we knew we would be scrapping.

I remember one night in the Vine pub in Tenterden

when I was sixteen, I started a scrap over a game of pool. There was no need to but I was in that mood as usual. I accused the fella I was playing of cheating when he potted the black to beat me. He hadn't cheated but it seemed a good way to piss him off. Another scrap ensued and the reputation I was building was getting stronger with every week. I felt set free from all the fear that had dictated my young life.

To go from spending years feeling weak and unworthy of being on this planet, to suddenly having this power within me was impossible to control at times. I couldn't go back to those old feelings again; it had ripped me apart inside for too long.

At sixteen I managed to blag my way into a job at NatWest bank after promising them I would be getting great grades in my exams. They were fools for believing that!

I started the Monday after I finished school and managed to work for eighteen months before I lost the will to live; I couldn't stand being around so many bitchy women every day, five days a week. It was grinding on my happiness. It was a bloody awful job.

I was living a very dysfunctional life at that time; all my wages went on partying and not giving a fuck about anything other than getting out of my head. I had become a chameleon: I was one person when out and about and the caring son and brother at home.

I went into the bank one day and told the manager I had a doctor's appointment at two; I left and never went back. I was sat in the beer garden of the pub opposite the bank when they all walked out at five o'clock. What a piss taker I was. My manager's face was a picture when I raised my pint glass to him as he left the bank to head for his car; they never heard from me again.

I had a penchant for weed, alcohol and speed which, in hindsight, was not a great mix. But at the time it was a concoction that guaranteed my sparkling personality would stay intact. For years, drugs and drink became my tactic for masking the real hurt that was going on under the armour.

I ended up dossing on a mate's sofa as I didn't want my Mum to see the mess I was becoming. She had done such an amazing job bringing me up I didn't want her to feel it was her fault that I was acting out in such a destructive manner.

I spent years thinking everyone was giving me the eye or being aggressive towards me. Over the years, I learnt they were just reflecting the attitude and anger I projected to the world.

The next couple of years disappeared into a mist of working hard and partying hard which all came to a crescendo when I beat up that guy outside the pub.

As I said in the introduction, that night scared the shit out of me. Who had I become? It has taken years to come to terms with the answer to that question, because what I had created is exactly what I had spent the first fourteen years of my life detesting. I had become a fucking bully. I spent years trying to justify my behaviour to myself and others by saying I only had fights with people who were bullies or full of themselves. What a crock of shit that was. I was looking to others to believe me, so I could feel better about myself.

I was in my early twenties and my reputation had been well and truly sealed. It is so easy to get a reputation but not so easy to get rid of it. Knowing I had turned into the thing I hated most just imprinted even more negativity into my psyche, leaving me with yet another mask to wear.

People knew if they came into the pub and I was there that it was going to be a session: we would drink too much, take too much ecstasy and laugh all weekend.

I had some of the best times of my life during that period: I made mates for life and we did some crazy arse shit. That I don't regret.

But there was always an undercurrent flowing through me: I was bloody angry.

I had been angry at the world for the first fourteen years of my life, then I spent the next fourteen years being angry at myself. Anger bubbled beneath the surface like a fiery river running through my veins. It was confusing as I was having a great time in life but I knew there was a darkness there too.

Being on my own became a catalyst for negative thinking. I knew I was self-harming with the drugs and alcohol. I was self-harming in other ways too: if I staggered home on my own from a night out, I would scrape my knuckles along brick work just so I could feel the pain and see my blood. On too many occasions to remember, I thought about jumping in front of a car when walking home from the pub pissed, just to end the charade.

I was spending many a night on my own in my flat, drinking cheap wine and considering how empty my life was on the inside. I would sit there watching shit TV booing my eyes out, not from any particular thought; the tears would just come.

Over the years I had built myself into a human

pressure cooker. The nights drunk and crying on my own were my release, where no one could see what was really happening to me.

I was twenty-eight years old and for fourteen years had been living a life with no purpose or value. I had done jobs that didn't interest me at all. I had a string of shit relationships behind me (my parent's separation had instilled a belief no one lasted, so why bother?) I had been self-harming in a variety of ways for years. Drinking to excess, taking drugs to excess, starting fights with the hope of getting the shit beaten out of me and punching and scraping walls so that I bled.

I decided one day to go to Brighton for the weekend on my own, just to get some headspace and try to find a way to escape this dark cloud that seemed to be following me about. I thought a weekend away and a few beers would help me process things, find something that was missing.

I was on autopilot as I was driving, my mind consumed by thoughts. What they were I could not tell you.

Then I was in a car park, engine off, staring over the cliffs of Beachy Head. I knew it was famous for people committing suicide. I couldn't remember driving there and I didn't understand why I was there. Suicide had been in and out of my thoughts for ten years but I never really believed I would ever act on them thoughts.

I sat there for five hours looking over the cliffs contemplating my life, how little it meant, how I had spent so many years pretending. I did not know who I was.

It was so confusing because I knew that the last fourteen years had been brilliant fun. I had pushed my body to its limits with the number of drugs I took at times, I had mates that I knew would die for me, I had so many great memories of partying, not caring and living life without a thought to the future.

Then there was this soft, gentle soul who felt battered.

Like he had no hope, was lost in the whirlwind of pretending and did not know how to escape. I could not get the two parts of me to work together, to try and create a whole. I was like Jekyll and Hyde, two different people in one body.

I never saw myself as a violent young man, just an angry one who chose the simple way of showing the anger.

I remember wondering what it would be like to jump, what it would be like for this shadow to be lifted. The usual stuff: who would miss me? people would be better off without me; who would come to my funeral? do I drive the car off the edge or jump? What scared me the most was the fact that I had got there; I had not had any control over it. Part of me deep inside wanted me to be there, wanted me to consider ending my life. How hidden where my dark thoughts that someone could end up in this place with no control? It highlighted that I had felt deeply out of control for most of my life and that is a long time for anyone.

It was a bloody long few hours. I didn't step out of the

car once. Part of me was terrified that if I took that step, I would walk to the cliff edge and jump. I knew there was no time for change once you had jumped.

I started to notice things around me: the sky was a clear blue and the sun was shining. There weren't many people about, walkers or other people hanging around. It was peaceful in a macabre sense, the emptiness of it all but also the simple beauty of it.

I started to answer the questions I had asked myself earlier. Luckily, I have a family that love me to bits, warts, and all. I have friends who have always got my back. I thought that these people would be devastated if I took my life, which led to the seed being planted that I would be devastated at taking my own life.

Maybe there was worth in me staying alive, maybe the darkness would lift, maybe I could feel different.

This is what made me start my engine and carry on driving to Brighton, not a sense of 'I deserve better' but a sense that I could not do this to people I love. I couldn't do it to myself.

This idea grew over the next day into a sense of determination to change my own path, to let go of my negative thoughts and take control. I did a lot of thinking in Brighton the next day and decided I was going to make changes. If I did not want to get back to that darkness again, I needed to take control of my own choices. I did not have to keep following this path just because I had been on it so long.

I honestly believe now that I was drawn to Beachy Head to learn a lesson: the lesson of belief. I left that weekend believing my life could be different; my future did not have to match my past. The bumps in the road are part of the journey; they don't have to dictate the direction you are going.

This chapter was all about instilling a sense of belief in you, that your life can be different, that wherever your past has taken you, you can make changes.

Tip for everyday-

I want you to get friendly with the parts of you and your history that you have labelled as negative. Look at the things that have happened to you and start to change how you see it. This works with everything, trauma, anxiety, negative emotions, self-defeating behaviours and so much more.

You have already planted seeds if you have done the work set in the first chapters; it is now time for you to start growing and nurturing them. Becoming comfortable with the uncomfortable times in our lives forms a solid foundation for the seed to grow.

The aim of this chapter is to help you turn your programming around. Negative times in your life can become positives by accepting who you are in this moment, no matter what has gone before. I am a great believer that we learn the most through our negative life experiences. The secret is to not be afraid of them but to use those experiences to grow.

I also want you to regularly spend time just sat with you building up the belief you are in control of what comes next, that what has brought you to this point has served its purpose. Now it is your time to shine like the brightest star.

Task-

In lesson #3 I asked you to list your negative thought and behaviour patterns. I now want you to look back at that list and counteract it with the positives you could take from it such as the experience teaching you resilience, hidden strength, self-sufficiency, optimism that you will do things differently, hardiness, creativity and a thirst for knowledge to name just a few.

Further reading-

I recommend you read *Breaking the Habit of Being Yourself. How to Lose Your Mind and Create a New One* by Joe Dispenza. He talks about the science behind changing any aspect of your life but also teaches you tools to enable this. I am not a science guy at all but this guy has a way about him that is easy to understand and leaves you wanting to hear more.

Universal Lesson #8

You live a life full of achievements, be proud of

them.

There are already enough people in the world who will try and put you down, try and belittle your achievements. Do not be one of them.

There is a thing called negative bias which describes how, as humans, we find it easier to connect to negativity. This is believed to be evolutionary because in our early human history paying attention to dangerous and negative threats was a matter of life and death.

It is believed that in the first year we are born our attention goes from noticing positives to negativity, mainly because our brains have a greater response to negative stimuli. This, therefore, has an impact on how we make choices and the risks we are willing to take because we base a huge amount of our choices on external influences.

It is not externally we need to look, it is internally. From the day we are born we achieve things; yet we often ignore our triumphs because it is part of our DNA.

The above knowledge gives you an advantage because now you know that when you are leaning towards negativity it is a natural thing. It gives you the chance to reframe things, that adopting a more positive outlook on life is your choice. When you push away compliments or achievements you are cementing what has already been before, it is now time for you to decide, a positive or negative approach to life? Whatever you decide is the life you will lead.

Your life is full of achievements. That could be getting out of bed in the morning when you would rather hide away under the cover, giving birth to a child, being nice to the neighbour or finishing school or adult education.

There are so many, the list could be endless.

This chapter will help inspire you to start noticing your own achievements. It is not narcissistic to pat yourself on the back, if anything it is paramount that you do. This chapter also explores the power of the subconscious and how it tries to distract you from finding new superpowers because it likes to feel safe. The more YOU live consciously, the more you get to write your own story.

It was February 2014, one month into my big adventure. I had been staying for about two weeks in a little village called Pai in Northern Thailand. Within those two weeks I had become good friends with three fellas I had met at the Hotel Pailifornia (see what they did there, geniuses!).

After an adventurous day out on our 50cc mopeds, Frank, Len and myself decided we would go to our favourite bar and treat ourselves to what we felt was the best Thai green curry in Thailand, whilst Peter stayed back at the hotel to rest.

We sat there eating, drinking and having a good laugh

over the day's adventures. Then the lads started to talk about some of the things they had done in life; it was inspiring stuff.

I then dropped my own story into the conversation. 'I attempted to climb Kilimanjaro two years ago.'

'What do you mean attempted to? What happened?' Frank asked with real interest in his voice.

'Not much to say, really lads,' I replied, not totally sure I was comfortable with speaking about the experience now that I had dropped it into conversation.

They both seemed to be genuinely interested in finding out what happened. 'We'd love to hear what happened, Mark,' Len said again.

So, I started to explain what had gone on.

'I used to work for a charity alongside running my private counselling business,' I said. 'I helped young people without any life skills or family support.' I found myself looking at them to see how they were reacting to my words and they both sat there listening attentively. 'I found it hard that these youngsters thought their lives would always be like

this, hard work, living on the edge of society and not being

able to follow their dreams. I wanted to prove to them that

anything is achievable with hard work, determination and a

passion to do your absolute best.'

'What did your workplace think of your idea?' one of

the lads asked.

'I remember sitting in my manager's office explaining

to him what I wanted to do and why. I was committing to

something I wasn't even sure I could do but it was out in the

open and the charity was supportive of my crazy idea.'

I felt like I was holding myself back from getting to the

meat of the story, but I also wanted to point out to the lads my

lack of physical fitness. 'I'd just turned thirty-seven years old;

I was four stone overweight, smoked too much and hadn't

done any regular exercise since I gave up football in my early

thirties. I totally blagged the training I was supposed to be

doing, which just left me full of doubts over whether I would succeed at what seemed an outrageous challenge.'

'How much training did you do?' Frank asked.

'I went for three walks around some local hills and lost about a stone in weight. That was it.' I felt ashamed saying it out loud.

'But you didn't cancel or back out of it?'

'Was too late. I'd made the commitment and before I knew it the day to leave was in front of me.'

'So how was it? Stop holding back, tell us about the climb,' Frank said with a smile.

I decided in that moment that I was just going to tell them everything.

'It was a strange experience gents. From day one I knew I was fucked. Walking in that heat was horrendous and I was never going to be able to make it. But I pretended everything was fine. I even lit up cigarettes on the rest stops.'

Len and Frank were still listening intently, so I just carried on. 'I had, by this point, made firm friends within the group and the camaraderie between us was what got me through those first four days. People were starting to open up about their own reasons for doing the trek and the anxieties they had about it. I remember thinking thank fuck I'm not the only one anxious about the climb.'

'That's a natural way to think,' Len put forward, sensing my discomfort.

'When we got to the huts that we'd be using as base to do the summit climb my body and mind were all over the show, I was pretty sure I wasn't going to make it to the summit. Of course, it was all my own fault so I was beating myself up viciously about my lack of preparation.

'We were going to do an acclimatisation trek up the first part of the summit just to make sure everyone was alright with it, up to this point we hadn't had anyone with adverse reactions to the altitude. As we were getting ready to do this little two-hour trek a ruckus erupted around us. We all stood there giving each other quizzical looks, what the heck was going on? Then, from down the side of the mountain, came four Sherpas pulling a stretcher with one wheel in the middle – I'm guessing to help get it over the terrain. Laid in it was some fella who was wrapped up in sheets and did not look good. We found out afterwards that the altitude had got to him and he had collapsed. Watching this unfold in front of us was the last thing we needed to see before we headed off to do our own summit climb the next day.'

Len and Frank looked horrified, although not a patch on how I looked at the time.

'My language towards myself wasn't helping me. How the fuck was I going to get up there tomorrow? This bloke looked fit, young and healthy. I knew as I got back to the huts that my mind had caught up with my failing body: tomorrow was going to be impossible. I felt so deflated.'

You could see the lads were feeling worried about where I was going with the story but they didn't say anything, just sat silently waiting for me to carry on. So, I decided to tell the whole story of summit night in one hit.

'We left at eleven at night and we formed a line to start the trek upwards. I had my small day rucksack on my back filled with water, a little bit of chocolate and a whole lot of trepidation. My rucksack felt like it weighed forty kilos rather than the five it realistically weighed. Looking at the faces around me I saw excitement, nervousness and lots of blank expressions as if people were in their own world of expectation and anxiety.

We had about twenty local guides with us that would be walking with us to the summit. These guys were phenomenal, fit as a butcher's dog. As we took our first steps on this crazy endeavour they started to sing, this made everyone smile in the group, even me. I found the song really uplifting, I remember thinking to myself maybe this wouldn't be so bad after all.

But within an hour I felt like my whole world was falling apart, my walking boots felt like lead blocks on the end of a pair of spaghetti legs, the rucksack was now feeling as if I had another person on my back. The start of the climb was on a hill of slate. It was soul destroying. Every two steps you took forward you slipped back one; I had walked for an hour nonstop and felt like I had covered about ten metres. I wasn't going to get to the top; I knew this at that moment. I grabbed Sarah, the young girl from the tour group who had organised the whole ten days, and said "I have to stop; I can't keep going. I'm going back." Sarah, bless her, kindly replied, "That doesn't sound like you, Mark. Get your head down and keep going. You'll get there."

It seemed that somewhere along the journey I had given the impression I was smashing it. But it did stick and I realised I'm not one for giving up that easily, so I decided to get my head down and just do one step at a time.

I had a guide who had attached himself to my side. He could obviously see I was struggling. He asked me if he could carry my rucksack. I had already seen others hand theirs over to a guide but for some reason I couldn't do it. Carrying it had become part of the challenge.

I plodded on for another half hour, dragging one foot after another, feeling the slate slide every time I put my foot down. I was wearing so many layers as it was bloody freezing but I was sweating underneath as if I was on a tropical beach. As I looked up, I remember seeing the group pulling away. I didn't have anyone close to me, well other than my very patient guide, who was smoking a fag, unbelievable. I had to give myself a chance so I asked my guide to take my rucksack. This was so hard and did not leave my thoughts for the rest of the climb up and the descent down, I felt a weaker man for handing it over. However, it did take some of the unbearable weight off me. Not enough because there was still my eighteen stone to carry up and the weight of my negative thoughts that were weighing me down more than anything.

I reached the first stop point. It had taken me so long that as I was arriving people were getting up after they had rested to start the next part of the climb. This was quite demotivating as it just ingrained the fact I was trailing behind. But I knew I had to get my mind working.

I needed a drink, so we ordered another round before I continued with what was turning into quite a cathartic experience.

I spent ten minutes at this break getting some water in me and a small bit of chocolate but mostly I gave myself a positive talking to. I would get to the top if it were the last thing I would do. I had to pull away from the fact my ego had attached to all these negatives. I had to accept I wasn't as fit as the others; my body had nothing left. It wasn't a race, my manhood wouldn't become less if I wasn't first to the top, you know I had to overcome all that ego-orientated bullshit that holds us back at times.'

I could even feel myself getting angry as I told the story back.

'The next part was more of a climb. Over rocks,

between rocks, I may have even crashed through the middle of a few. It was pitch black and there was only a few of us climbing together, as most of the group were off at their own pace. We had to get to Gilman's point, which was at 5681 metres high. The few hours it took to get there were the toughest I have ever experienced. I was battered from banging against rocks, slipping and twisting in ways my body was not designed for. But we made it. Daylight had started to appear at some point and the views were becoming spectacular.'

I paused here because I had to decide about how honest I wanted to be with these new mates of mine that were hanging on my every word. As I'd been recollecting this tale to them, I knew this was my opportunity to let go of the baggage I had been carrying since the climb.

'Right lads, I've got to take you back to the first stop point we had. I was messed up, angry and frustrated. It was at this point that when we stood up to carry on walking the tears arrived, I couldn't stop them. Luckily, my face was virtually covered with woolly hats and a snood so only I knew. Twenty years ago, my anger would have moved me to fight someone else but I couldn't really go around Kilimanjaro fighting Sherpas; I would need them. Plus, they would kick the shit out of me and I was in enough pain already. So my anger came out in tears, hours of fucking tears.'

I looked at Peter and Frank expecting a chortle of laughter or an embarrassed look out the window but I didn't get any of that. I got two of the kindest faces I had ever seen just silently keeping eye contact with me, quietly without words just letting me know it was alright.

The restaurant we were in seemed empty, as if it were just the three of us sat there. I was feeling emotional by now. I had never told anybody about the tears, I didn't want anyone to see me as weak for spending six hours crying to myself, whilst avoiding eye contact with anyone coming back down after summiting.

'I just wanted to sit down and admire the sunrise

coming above the clouds or the views over the valleys that were overlooked by the majestic Kilimanjaro but I just kept being pushed by my fucking cigarette-smoking, constantly smiling Sherpa.

'I saw the summit, oh bollocks, no I didn't because when I got there it was one of them false summits. Who even knew they existed? No one warned me, the bastards. But thirty minutes later I saw the sign, Uhuru Peak, 5895 metres.

'This is going to sound silly I know but all I could think was, I don't like the new sign they have to mark the summit. The old wooden sign had been replaced by a new,

bright green, plastic-looking thing. Shocking decision Kilimanjaro council, they need to have a revote.

'I stood in front of that sign and I have never felt such a sense of relief in my entire life. Funnily enough, I had run out of tears by then so no one saw them when I took off my hat and snood for the obligatory summit photo. Funny that, hey?'

'But then I got rushed to turn around and start the descent down. It had taken so long for me to get up there they were worried about time. I wanted to stand there and breathe it all in: the awesome glacier sat there at the top of the world; the view of what seemed like the whole world; the icy wind blowing against my face letting me know I was still alive. But we had to go. It seemed like a lot of hard work just to get ten minutes at the top.

'It must have been minus fifteen at the summit but the sun was coming out and I was hopeful for the easier jaunt back down the side of the mountain. The only problem was my legs had nothing left, although my mind was feeling extremely positive after I had managed to drag myself to the summit kicking and screaming.

'As I descended it got hotter and hotter, my layers of clothing starting to feel like a hindrance. I was dehydrated, starving hungry, tired and emotional. I managed to get to the place where we had our first stop on the way up, after that it all went a bit pear shaped for my elastic legs.

'Two minutes after leaving the stop place, I stepped down from some rocks only for my right leg to give way. It had nothing left; any strength had been replaced by lead. So I crumbled to a pile of worn-out flesh laying on jagged rocks. After a few swear words, my guide came over and offered me his hand which I accepted and got back up. Twenty steps later I was sat on my arse again, my temper getting more explosive with every fall. There were lots of expletives and angry words with myself, sticks being thrown in frustration and an all-round dark cloud over my head. Again and again I fell for over an hour. Eventually the guide learnt to keep his distance and just let me get on with it; he even looked a bit scared at times as if I was going to chuck him off the side of the mountain in a fit of rage, poor lad. But the anger I was letting out was making me stand up again. I was not having it. For some strange reason, at that moment, my mind felt stronger than it had for the whole climb. So the falls kept happening and the cuts kept growing but my feet kept moving.

'When we got to the slate part of the descent, I told my guide he could leave me. It was easy to see the way back down and I was pretty sure it had been a traumatic experience following me. He'd been by my side for over twelve hours, what a star!

'Slate is a lot easier to walk down than it is to walk up. Before he left, my guide told me to run straight as a dye down it, I had seen others from the group doing it in front of me. The fear of falling didn't exist anymore as I had spent the last few hours practicing so much, so I thought sod it, why not? It was fun. I had no control over my body; I would manage to stay up for a bit then fall and roll get back up and repeat.

'The final half hour was the easiest part of the last twelve hours; I had my rucksack back on and I was down to a t-shirt. I staggered into camp on legs that made me look like a new-born calf, all wobbly and no strength. Henk and Sarah were standing there ready to congratulate me on succeeding. I walked straight past them to the back of the huts. I leant against the wall and slithered down it to the ground, where I put my head in my hands and cried a little bit more, it was uncontrollable. The seesaw of emotions just kept flooding out, the relief, the anger and more relief.'

I had to let go of everything at this point and I couldn't have wished for two better men to share this moment with. 'So that's the pitiful story.'

'What do you mean?'

'OK so I got to the top, but it didn't really count.'

Why the bloody hell not?' Frank asked me.

'Because I gave my rucksack away for someone else to carry and I cried for much of the climb.' I had never said those words out loud before.

'You're fucking kidding me, right? So, you walked for thirteen hours, after wanting to quit after one. You had no physical strength in your whole body and you felt like your mind was an empty vessel? But you made it to the top of

Kilimanjaro and back down again! What an amazing feat of mind over body. Give yourself a break, mate.'

In that moment, the tiny little parasite that had eaten away at me for the last two years evaporated in the unassuming little bar with Frank and Len.

My man ego had been dented by the act of handing over my bag and my honest tears. I couldn't believe it took me so long to accept this inspiring achievement. So thank you Frank and Len for allowing me to dump a huge rucksack of baggage. The baggage I had carried for so many years was about me not carrying my own baggage. It is so ironic that now it just makes me smile away to myself.

Now when I talk about Kilimanjaro, I praise myself and speak openly about the tears and the rucksack. Considering where I was physically it was an unbelievable accomplishment.

Noticing your achievements is a fantastic way of

changing your internal view of yourself, the smallest of achievements should be noticed every day.

Now, as an adult, you have a choice what to carry forward. If you want your story to be different, grab a pen and rewrite it.

Tip for everyday-

Most people when they look back on their life will pick out their regrets, things they wish they had done differently. Looking back and discovering all the amazing achievements you have made can be liberating.

We are fascinatingly complex beings, like puzzles that constantly change. Recognising and accepting your achievements builds confidence, self-awareness and control.

Control, this is what YOU are aiming for. Control of your thoughts and actions so YOU can create a life well lived.

Task-

It is hard to give yourself time but this is what I want

you to do. At the end of each day, consciously take the time to think about what you achieved that day, giving it time is what will change your programming.

Try not to get wrapped up in the idea that an achievement must be massive, like I have said, the smallest of recognised achievements can make huge changes. You are starting to build up a portfolio of positivity towards yourself, be kind to yourself.

Don't forget to put what comes up in the journal notes, it will continue to be a great way for you to reflect on your journey.

Further Reading-

There is a wonderful film on YouTube by Patrick Solomon called *Finding Joe*; it is wonderfully put together. It shows the power of taking the heroes journey, which you are all on.

Universal Lesson #9

We are the bearers of our own suffering.

We are the bearers of our own pain; we hang on to negative thoughts and desires that keep us on a path of suffering. There are tough times in life; it is an inevitable part of living. Being able to get yourself to a point where you can accept the good and the bad that will happen in your life gives you opportunity, an opportunity to consciously take the power back.

Too many times I have heard, it has always been like this so it always will be. Just because it is easier to sit in old habits doesn't mean you should. Be honest with yourself, it is time to accept the shit that has happened in your life and use it for your own purpose.

YOU

However, be careful because we can swap old negative patterns for new ones then congratulate ourselves for moving forward. Months or years down the line we notice we have not moved forward at all, we've just exchanged the issue for a different one, nicely keeping us in our comfort zone.

Without honesty, awareness and acceptance your new negatives will have been embedded in your everyday routine, which can then lead to another few years of not living your best life.

You see, your subconscious wants to keep you safe and it will do this by keeping you in old habits that have created believable safe thoughts and behaviours.

Take the five-year-old kid that gets barked at by the big, scary dog. Adults around them reinforce that dogs are dangerous and they should be avoided because they have let their fear dictate their response.

140

This may leave the kid so terrified of dogs that when they are twenty and a gentle, docile and friendly dog approaches them in the park, they panic, get anxious and leave the situation. The subconscious then tells the twenty-year-old that was the only way to keep them safe.

This belief carries on growing and growing over the years, causing anxiety and fear of situations. So coping mechanisms are put in place, they avoid places they do not know and keep away from all animals just in case.

All this shit because the subconscious believes it is keeping you safe based on the details it has been shown. It's very clever a lot of the time and much needed. Within our negative thoughts and behaviours is programming that needs changing so that we can see the world through different eyes.

Imagine if one of the parents had explained that not every dog is like that and that a dog could even be a best friend who would always look out for this kid. They might describe how some dogs are not friendly and point out how to recognise dogs and their behaviours. This would have saved years of anxiety and fear.

So just because your subconscious plants a programme to protect you at one point in your life does not mean that this will be the same for the rest of your life.

As you are now aware I used drink and drugs for a variety of reasons: to avoid what was below the surface, to fit in and not be alone, and mainly to give my emotions a safe place to sit.

At the top of Beachy Head, I had to decide whether to carry on or call an end to the charade of my life. That decision was to go on and it took me on an amazing, uncertain path to where I am now.

I stopped being a labourer and managed to get my foot in the door of the care industry. I was loving being able to give something back, to be able to use my own life experience to make a difference. It was looking rosy.

Then in my early thirties I started to notice a new way

of thinking that was making me feel shit about myself. Whenever I walked past shop windows and saw myself reflected, I hated what I was seeing. This gave my critical voice the opportunity to come running back into my life.

Somehow over the three years since Beachy Head I had put on a ridiculous amount of weight; I had reached twenty-two stone.

You see when I took away the calming, "safe" influences of alcohol and drugs my emotions had no safe place to stay. So, without realising, my subconscious brought in another coping mechanism: emotional eating.

I would secretly eat when I was sad, angry, lonely or whenever I felt any of the emotions that I had kept at bay with drink and drugs. My subconscious thought it was better for me to hide away from these raw emotions rather than face up to them. Whilst I was patting myself on the back for getting control of my old habits, the sneaky little fucker added a new one.

That was not the end of the similarities between my old and new behaviours; when I was abusing my body with drink and drugs there would always be a reckoning, a moment in time when it would all come crashing down around me, leaving me feeling shit about myself, full of shame and regret.

My subconscious kindly attached the same outcome to my newfound eating habits, so when I became aware that I had an eating problem along came the shame and regret at allowing myself to be so easily directed. Wallop There you have it: another negative thought and behaviour pattern to replace my old ones. What a bitch.

Once I had realised that eating had become an issue for me, I used that awareness to put certain things in place and they worked most of the time. When I left to go on my travels, I felt like I was in a good place with my eating issues.

This all came crashing down around me at the end of my second week travelling, when I was making my way to

Sukhothai from Kanachanubri via Bangkok in Thailand. I spent the day squeezing into trains, tuk-tuks and buses. I was hot, tired and open to criticism.

All day it had played on my mind. Were people saying 'look at that fat, old boy trying to look like he is capable of travelling the world.' I was sat in this tiny tuk-tuk driving into town reinforcing all the negative beliefs I had. My language sounded like my old school bully.

I had decided not to book anywhere to stay ahead of my arrival as I was still desperate to release as many constraints as possible. I thought playing it by ear would add another little bit of risk and adventure to my arrival in Sukhothai.

If I told you that it took me two hours to find somewhere to stay you will understand that my bright idea of being so resourceful started to bug me. Every hostel and hotel I tried was fully booked; not such a sleepy town after all. I managed, in the end, to get a room in a hotel, a very posh, big room with a warm shower and a bed was just right. I didn't even mind that it cost me so much, well about a tenner!

By the time I got into my room I was in a shocking mood. It had been a long, hot and uncomfortable day travelling and I arrived with a big dark cloud hanging over me. All my awareness and coping mechanisms had fucked off, leaving me feeling like I was sat in a hotel room full of Kryptonite.

I was so fed up; I just wanted to hide from the world. I got even more pissed off with myself for not being able to control this behaviour. I ended up doing exactly what was making me feel shit in the first place. I ate and I ate. Room service made a few quid off me that afternoon!

I was sat in my hotel room, in my boxers feeling disgusted at what I saw in the mirror, having eaten too much and my thoughts full of self-loathing.

I couldn't snap out of it. All my logical thinking had disappeared into the ether. I couldn't get my head around not having an effing clue what I was doing. I was all alone in this strange country not knowing the language or their way of living. What the hell was I doing? I should grow up and go home and accept the life of an overweight, middle-aged man.

From somewhere I came up with the great idea of mixing my old negative behaviour with the new one, so I decided to go out and get pissed. Because if overeating weren't going to solve it, then of course getting pissed would make it all clearer, bloody subconscious!

I was sat at a table on my own, staring into my second pint of lager. Thinking I was going to drown the thoughts out with strong Thai beer and just wallow in my own shit, this Superhero was having a fucking day off.

What was pissing me off more than anything as I sat there: I know how the mind works. I know how my mind works; I teach others to stay aware of their own choices. I have a huge amount of awareness where my eating habits are concerned. Here I was, slumped over a table, pissed off, getting pissed and I wasn't using the array of skills that I had at my disposal. That was just another excuse for my critical voice to take control, rather than me using it as a springboard for change in that moment.

'Excuse me do you mind if I sit down?' I heard from behind me.

'Of course, I fucking mind. Can't you see I'm wallowing in self-pity here?' is what I grumpily said inside my head. What came out of my mouth was, 'Of course mate, grab a chair.'

'Cheers. I saw you sitting on your own from my table over there and thought I would come and say hi.' This stranger said to me in some strange accent with a huge, bloody smile on his face.

'What the fuck has he got so much to smile about?' Again, my inner voice did not match my external voice. 'Do you fancy a beer?' I asked in my best pretend friendly voice.

'Go on then,' he jovially replied.

'So, what brings you to Thailand?' he asked with what came across as genuine interest.

'I gave up my job, my home and put all the money I have into one bank account, so I can go and see the world. It seemed like a good idea at the time.'

'Does it not now? Because that is an amazing thing to do, much the same as what I have done. I have been travelling around Asia for six months now and have had an absolute amazing time.'

I won't go into the whole two-hour conversation, but I will tell you this guy was full of positive energy. We talked about what it was like travelling alone, how they lived in Thailand and having a chuckle.

It was just what I needed. Somehow when you're down, if you notice the signs, you can be lifted right back up.

My slumber gently lifted and I allowed myself to take on board the compliments. I invested in the conversation and could feel my own energy and thoughts coming in line with his. It was a moment within my travels that had a huge impact even to this day. I haven't allowed myself to get to that point of self-flagellation since and will forever be grateful to that Finnish guy for reminding me that our subconscious does not have to rule our present.

Can you remember a time when you have not been at your best, then someone has come along and cracked a joke or told you what you need to hear? Can it be coincidence or is it a higher level of spirituality telling us not to give up or that life could always be worse? I don't have the answers but what I can tell you is that when I need a lift I normally get one, as long as I take notice of the small things around me and stop worrying about the things I can't control.

I left the pub that night feeling positive, energised and silly for allowing my old nemesis, my weight, dictate my enjoyment of this adventure. I got back to the hotel ready for a nice sleep and excited for the day ahead. I knew the walls where thin when I could hear the people in the room next door put the shower on and I then spent some time listening to them having quick sex. Luckily the bloke was not much of a stallion, so I did manage to get off to sleep that night!

I want to let you know it is alright to have moments when you are not completely in control of your subconscious. Even with all I have learnt there are huge amounts of time when I forget to apply the lessons.

That night in Thailand I had stopped accepting myself: my weight, the way I looked, the choice I made to travel. I allowed old thoughts to make me believe I wanted to be how I had always been. It's tough to sit back and honestly say to yourself that you are making choices you know will make you unhappy, but if you want permanent change, you must be brutally honest with yourself every day.

I believe life is not about how many times you get knocked down; it is about how many times you get back up. The foundations of who we are will be built off our moments of hardship. Our strengths are embedded when we are resilient to whatever that life throws at us.

Tip for everyday-

Be aware of your subconscious and its power to replace one negative behaviour with another. If you meet the change with honesty and awareness, it has no power.

Use the skills you have developed throughout this book. Use your awareness and your bravery to carry on writing your own story.

When you are on this journey it will sometimes feel overwhelming and too much hard work to keep moving forward, but the universe is there to help you along the way. Everyone has a friendly Finnish guy just waiting to turn up when times are tough. Noticing these moments and taking from them is hugely powerful.

The subconscious feeds off laziness so you need to be consistently taking action, re-cementing all you learn. My biggest downfalls within everyday life are when I get lazy with my mind and body. Stay awake in your own life, it will lead to magical moments.

You can have all the self-awareness in the world but if **YOU** don't **ACT** on that awareness, you just stay in the life you are already in.

Task-

How do you create your own suffering? What habits do you have that make you feel shit? What stops you from taking action to change them?

I understand a lot of this is going over topics already spoken about, but this is to help you create a clearer, honest picture of the things holding you back. Habits are formed by repetition, so the more you reflect and give the areas of your life you want to change the attention they need, the easier it becomes to take the action to change them.

Look for the signs in your everyday life, the little things that have the power to put a smile back on your face. If you are the one in a great mood, then smile. It's contagious.

Further Reading-

Try reading *The Art of Happiness* by The Dalai Lama.

Buddhism talks a lot about us creating our own suffering.

Universal Lesson #10

Learn from others who are on their superhero

journey.

The universe surrounds us with inspiring people and stories; if you want to change your own path learn from others.

Surround yourself with people and environments that make you want to be the best version of yourself, the superhero that is not scared to face his villains.

The data we give ourselves every day impacts how we live our lives, so step away from negative influences. Open your mind to the lessons that others have already learnt: be a student of the world.

Our mind is an ever-evolving entity, teach it the right lessons in life and it will develop into a wonderful tool for self-growth and happiness.

I spent my first thirty years creating a life that kept me in a cycle of self-destruction. It was fun at the time but was not good for me, physically or mentally.

The day I spent at the cliffs in Eastbourne was an awakening: something had to change. I did not want to distance myself from my mates, they were such a huge part of who I was, but I knew I needed to add another dimension to my everyday life.

When you start to take a new path there is a risk you forget that the old path is what has formed you up to that point. It is not a case of wiping it from your life but using the parts of it that can help you grow moving forward.

My mates always had my back. They were not the reasons for my shit choices. Why would I consider walking away from all they had given me? Even up to this day, I could not be who I am without my mates from the first thirty years of my life. I couldn't see any reason why that would change just because I was going to give another direction a go.

Even so, I started to connect with more spiritually minded people, joined a meditation group, made new friends and started to learn. I was a human sponge soaking up knowledge about the mind, spirituality and other simpler ways of living.

It was an amazing time in my life; I was starting to feel free. People like the Finnish guy would turn up in my life, teach me a valuable lesson then move on.

Don't get me wrong. It was early days so all the things that had dictated me for the first thirty years were still powerful, but for the first time I was fighting for it to be different.

This was when I realised that all the villains, I had created in my life externally, were in fact all parts of me.

When I started to surround myself with positivity, encouragement and creativity, the villains started to lose some of their hold over me.

Again, it was within my travels that I had my most powerful experience; this came from an unexpected source and it motivated me to work hard on becoming the superhero of my own life.

I arrived at Kanchanaburi on a hot January afternoon in 2014. I had no plans as to where I was going to stay or how long I would stay for.

I managed to find myself a lovely little hotel and at a tenner a night was a hidden gem. It had trees in the courtyard, little birds singing to me in the background and positive energies as soon as I walked into the open courtyard that the rooms were scattered around. The room was like a tent, with a shower that had some power to it. Happy days.

I had chosen Kanchanaburi because I had heard it was

where the film *Bridge Over the River Kwai* was based and I remember watching the film with my dad as a kid. Also, when I had stayed at the first hostel in Bangkok a few of the other travellers had recommended I go and see Hellfire Pass, which can be got to from Kanchanaburi.

The railway line was constructed by Asian labourers and Allied prisoners of war during the Second World War, it was part of the Burma railway which was aptly nicknamed the Death Railway. The working conditions were horrific, and the Japanese were cruel masters. It is estimated that sixty-nine men were beaten to death and many more died from cholera, dysentery, starvation, and exhaustion.

Hellfire Pass is so called because the sight of emaciated prisoners labouring at night by torchlight was said to resemble a scene from Hell. The railway was never built to last and with the bombing it suffered during the war it got closed; there are no longer any trains running on that stretch of the line. The nearest railway station is at Nam Tok Sai Yok Noi, where trains of the state railway of Thailand can be taken for a trip over the famous Whampo Viaduct and across the bridge over the River Kwai to Kanchanaburi.

It was a strange tour in many ways. I set out with the intention of not viewing it as a tourist. I knew there was something for me to learn on this tour although I wasn't sure what when I left my hotel.

I found myself very quickly detaching myself from the rest of the group when we started the tour, everyone just seemed to be whipping through without paying any attention to what was around them. They would take a few photos, listen to the guide for a minute then move on. I knew I was being judgemental that day but I couldn't help it.

You walk down a path, through a wood, before you come to the entrance of Hellfire Pass, where suddenly there is a rock face either side of you reaching up to thirty, forty feet; the walkway through is probably three metres wide. I felt shut in straight away, not in a claustrophobic way, but I could feel the history encompassing me.

I stood back from the group and let them move away, dutifully following the guide. There was a log on the path, so I sat on it and leant my back against the rockface. Shit me, it was like a giant rush through my body. I felt sad, tired and drained. It was like all the hurt and inhumane conditions these soldiers were made to suffer; I could feel.

I placed my hand on the rock face and was overwhelmed by the energy that poured into me. I felt sadness emanating through the rock. I must admit I had a tear in my eye for most of the trip, especially when I came across the plaques along the pass that described some of the atrocities that happened there, each accompanied by a beautiful bright red poppy.

I felt humbled to my core when it was time to leave, like I'd had a genuine life-changing experience. It also amazed me how much I had felt, not just in my head but also my physical reaction to being there. I cannot even begin to imagine what these men went through, how they felt or for those that survived the ordeal, the ever-lasting scars.

I spent the train ride back to Kanchanaburi in quiet contemplation, what an emotional few hours it had been.

There was a museum in the centre of town dedicated to the railway line and the prisoners of war that had worked on it, which I wanted to see the next day along with the huge graveyard opposite.

I have always believed that the human spirit is a thing to be held in high esteem but watching some of the films in the museum of POWs put a whole new meaning to the word. These guys were starved, worked tirelessly and treated like shit, but in all the pictures and films of the time, you can see them smiling and joking. As if saying to the enemy you can do what you like but you will not break me. I felt a sense of pride I had never felt before for a group of men I did not know.

I was in the museum for a couple of hours and it was

the most engaged I have ever been in a museum. I read private notes, watched a variety of films, held what they call trench art, art made from items of war to represent something other than pain and loss.

As I left the museum to walk across the road to the graveyard a darkness came over me, a sadness and an overwhelming desire to avoid it. I wanted to pay my respects to these strangers that had given up everything on the chance they could make a difference to others' lives. Bloody heroes all of them.

As you enter the graveyard there is a message carved into the side saying:

1939-1945

The land on which this cemetery stands is the gift of the Thai people for the perpetual resting place of the sailors, soldiers and airmen who are honoured here.

As I slowly meandered through the graveyard you could feel the respect of the Thai people that maintain it, there were five men working the grounds. Raking up leaves, trimming bushes, cleaning gravestones. I was taken aback by how it was kept; it looked immaculate. I had never seen such a pretty graveyard. The Thai people were obviously invested in keeping the memory of these men alive, even after seventy years. My respect for the Thai people grew a little bit more that day.

The graves were all in lines and every grave was adorned with bright flowers, clean and had messages beautifully inscribed on the plaques. As I stopped by graves to read the messages a pride emanated from me, pride in men who knew the real meaning of sacrifice. I stood by the graves of total strangers and cried, openly and without a thought of being judged by others as they paid their respects.

In lesson #4 I spoke about us being warriors, fighting for our best lives, but maybe this isn't the whole story. Maybe to be a true warrior you need to do more for others, that being selfless is just as much about fighting for others who can't as it is fighting for yourself.

These men and women gave their lives, for people they did not know. Their warrior spirit kept them fighting for these things when most people would crumble and give up.

It left me feeling that I had a responsibility to live my best life but also to help others live theirs.

When we have negative aspects within our lives, we tend to create an environment around us that keeps us nicely tucked up in its caring arms. We are drawn to negative people and situations because it allows our subconscious to confirm this is the safest place for us. It creates this internal world on previous experiences where it fitted but not all your subconscious protective beliefs are still relevant.

To live a different life, you must change parts of your existing one.

Tip for everyday-

Surround yourself with positive people and experiences. Find people who motivate you to be the best version of yourself.

Fill up your daily routine with positive influences, watch motivational videos, read books that teach you how to grow. Join a group of likeminded people; do not be scared to ask questions.

The world is full of people that have come from the depths of despair to create a magical world for themselves, learn from them and then become one of them..

All of life's magic is in your hands.

Start to create a world full of positivity. Take time to look at your friendship group, your home, your family and become aware of how they make you feel. Simplify and cleanse your life of toxic influences and see yourself flourish.

Task-

I want you to build a library of positive books, videos,

and people. List the ones you have come across already that you have connected to, then go and find new ones.

Are there any groups near where you live that you could join? If so, take action and join, if you don't enjoy the group, nothing is lost just try another one. It is your journey so what inspires you is individual to you, go explore.

Further Reading-

Have a look on YouTube and see how people like Sylvester Stallone and Keanu Reeves got to where they are.

Universal Lesson #11

Finding ways to connect to the present moment will lighten the burdens you carry.

There is a magical tool at our fingertips which has been used for thousands of years to create a positive life.

All the topics I have spoken about throughout this book can be reinforced by using this skill. All the areas you are struggling with and all the areas you want to expand on will benefit.

This chapter will help direct you towards a personal attribute that will get you off autopilot and encourage you to live a more conscious life. When you are more aware of each passing moment, you become available to appreciate the joy in life.

If you had come up to me twenty years ago and said, 'Hey Mark do you fancy doing some meditation or come on a mindful walk around the wood with me?' I would have laughed in your face and followed that with some not-so-polite piss taking.

I believed that all that stuff was for hippy wasters who didn't have anything better to do with their time. I mean, why would you sit in one spot for an hour with your legs crossed unnaturally whilst chanting Om, in the hope that it would solve all your life's problems? What a crock of shit.

I assumed that life just pulled you along in the direction it wanted to; you didn't have any choice as to where you were heading.

My fondness for ecstasy was an unconscious attempt at embracing the moment but it was not my reality. As a matter of fact, it kept me hidden away from the wonderful moments that could have been. The alcohol and drugs kept me so far away from living the moment, that eventually every moment for over a decade was a blur.

I don't remember how meditation started to become part of my life, but I do know that at the beginning it was a hard slog. I had masked everything for years and meditating brought a lot of it to the forefront of my thoughts; it was uncomfortable and scary at times.

But mixed in with these moments were magical moments of clarity, moments where my history did not dictate my thoughts and behaviours.

I met my friend, Sue, in my early thirties and she had a huge impact on my view of meditating and my confidence to do it. She was a spiritual teacher and supported people to grow their confidence within a more spiritual lifestyle. This led to me joining meditation groups and opening myself up to the unbound possibilities that this view of the world offered.

Lots of people seemed to look to these groups to direct their lives completely, which was not what I was looking for. Plus, with most groups there were internal politics, this eventually led me to walk away from the groups.

I will always be grateful for my time learning from Sue and the people in that circle but I wanted to learn as I went. I didn't want my choices in life to be dictated by spirits or other people. I was feeling confident enough in my skills and instinct that I knew I could walk my own path.

Meditation and mindfulness have become an integral part of my life. I have even qualified to become a teacher of it, with amazing results for others.

It is easy to talk to people who have tried meditation about the benefits of it because they have experienced them. It is people who are like my old self who are tougher because without actually experiencing something you always have to judge on what others tell you.

Below is a moment from my travels across Nepal that highlights the power of meditation. This is coming from a man who carried so much baggage that internally I walked like a haggard old witch. With practice, determination and maybe a few tears, I got to this magical point in my life.

My alarm was set for four-fifteen in the morning. (Yes, in the morning. Who would have thought there are two four-fifteens in the day? Not me.) I had organised a taxi to take me to the World Peace Pagoda that sat atop the hills surrounding Lake Phewa in Pokhara. It looked magnificent from the ground, shining in white as it seemingly protected the town of Pokhara that sat below its watching eyes. My idea was to get up there to see the sunrise over the lake and the Annapurna Mountain range, with the intention of just sitting quietly with myself for as long as was comfortable for me.

I stumbled around in the dark for half an hour in the pitch black, trying to follow the shocking direction the taxi driver had given me. I eventually found a few benches scattered around the top of the cliff which were away from the main pagoda site; it felt like the perfect place to sit. But to be fair it was my instinct I was following because my view was extremely limited. I could have been facing a rockface twenty metres in front of me for all I knew.

The darkness was replaced by clouds, and lots of them, but it didn't dampen my enthusiasm because I knew that even if I didn't get to see the sunrise, I would get an amazing view once the day started coming alive.

I hadn't given much time to meditating since being away so wanted to treat my time atop this mountain as time just for me, look for some answers and embrace just being me.

The first two hours were spent watching the clouds partly lift and the scene below opening up to me. WOW, what a view; one that will be imprinted on my mind forever. I was surrounded by flowers of the most beautiful colours, yellows, purples, and reds hit your eyes like laser beams, it was astonishing.

The whole scene was picture perfect, more than anything I had hoped for when I had considered coming up here. I didn't need the sunrise to value the experience I was having; it was as if this had been made just for me, a special gift for me to treasure for eternity.

The slow lifting of the clouds mirrored the gentle rise of calmness I was feeling within me. The clouds tenderly started to release the snow-capped peaks of the Annapurna mountains right in front of me. As time went by Phewa lake started to show its mystical life-giving form, the mountains reflecting in its clear water duplicating the beauty that it was surrounded by.

I don't see myself as a master of meditation and I found myself being self-conscious that morning at times, my mind acting up every time it heard something. I would open my eyes so I didn't look like a prat sat on the side of a mountain with his eyes closed. It was always nothing, as I was the only one that thought it would be a great idea to sit here and watch the world come alive. As time went on these interruptions into my thoughts became less and less.

The clarity of thought I found that morning was like a

pure, clear river running through my mind, it had the odd rock in it but nothing I could not traverse past.

Within the next four hours, I saw a friendly leather-faced Peruvian man in my mind. He made me feel like he was supporting me, as if he were putting an imaginary arm around my shoulders and saying *you are on the right path.* I saw an American Indian, as he sat on top of his huge white stallion with his spear, atop another mountain; he instilled a sense of protection within me.

There were points of nothingness which I had not experienced much before, it felt amazing. If you can imagine all your past anxieties and your future worries dissolving like ice in the sun, this is what it was like. My inner self was growing, I was not sure into what but I knew it was growing. I was noticing things that I would usually ignore: the wind on my face, the smell in the air, the colours of the grass and flowers and especially the clouds. Even now, clouds are a great source of calmness when I am letting days get on top of me.

Those hours sat above Phewa Lake made me feel more alive than ever and I had not done anything other than sit with myself. Six hours I ended up sat on my bench looking out across Pokhara; I did not get bored once. I did not look at the time and at no point did I think I should be somewhere else.

When you have spent most of your life just being pulled along by the universe with the sense of having no control, it starts to become monotonous at times and you lose your light, the fire in your belly. Mine was roaring like it was being powered by a giant set of bellows. I was feeling more energized and driven than ever before. I had a sense that I was taking control, that my mission to fight for my own choices was going better than I had ever anticipated. I was starting to become the superhero of my own life.

All we really have is this exact moment. The moment you are sat there reading this. Nothing else matters unless you give it power, this realisation is life changing.

In this moment, your past has no power because you have chosen to learn from it and not be driven by it. The fears for the future that you carry around like a debilitating weight on your shoulders no longer seem so heavy. You have faith in yourself so whatever is put your way you know you can deal with it.

My life and millions of other people's lives have been transformed by meditation, mindfulness and living in the moment.

Tip for everyday-

Get yourself off autopilot; notice everything around you. Your senses are a wonderful way to connect to the present moment. You cannot be anywhere else if you are consciously using one of your senses.

Go out into the world and smell, taste, feel, touch and listen as much as you can. Take an everyday object you would normally not give the time of day, sit down and notice it, breathe and see things you have never noticed before.

When you are consciously in the present moment you have the power of choice: how you think, how you react and how you make your decisions.

Task-

Start to meditate. Ask advice from someone you know who already does, find a local meditation group, join groups online, read about it.

But most important of all, don't criticise yourself whilst starting this process. Be kind, be aware, put in place all you have learnt and have fun.

Further Reading-

Take some time to read *The Power Of Now* by Eckhart Tolle. It's a fantastic depiction of the benefits of living the moment.

Universal Lesson #12

Be grateful for what you already have.

This will be the number one tool in your armoury as it will bring a simple beauty to the life around you. You start to become happy with what you already have rather than always searching for more in your life.

Daily gratitude will humble you and make you a kinder person; you will want to share your gratitude with the people around you. You are already surrounded by things and people to be grateful for but maybe you don't see them through the fog of everyday life. You don't need to surround yourself with stuff, possessions or people to get a sense of happiness or security in your life.

In fact, quite the opposite is true: the simpler you make your life the more secure and wonderful your life will become.

Unfortunately, we live in a consumerism society where we are easily distracted towards the next thing we can buy. This takes away the beauty of seeing all the magical things you are already surrounded by.

Have you ever heard the quote 'The best things in life aren't things? These are such a powerful few words. The truth is, when you are lying on your deathbed you will be talking about the adventures you have had, the risks you have taken, the people you have loved, the people you still love and the moments of joy and happiness you experienced.

It will not be your bank balance. So create memories not pound signs.

This whole book has been aimed at making you more conscious within your life, hopefully helping you to see what you already have so that you can let go of some of your negative attachments.

If you have put into place the universal lessons taught within this book you should have already started to simplify your life, finding it easier to recognise and appreciate the good people in your life, notice the positive moments and things you already have. You will be starting to become more comfortable with showing your appreciation externally to yourself and the world around you.

When I say simplify your life I don't mean give it all up to go and sit in a cave, whilst you live off crabs and seaweed. Oh no, what I mean is there will be things in your life that make it more complicated, stressful and out of your control. They are the things you need to let go of. Step away from them, take charge and be the boss of your own future.

We live in a world of overindulgence, where nothing is enough. This is hugely directed by technology, social media and the constant bombardment of society telling you that you must think a certain way, act a certain way and look a certain way.

The pressure this puts on us daily is massive. This then creates the anxiety, self-judgement and inferiority complex that a lot of the world live with all the time.

By following the book to this point, you should have started to create a clearer picture of how you want your life to be, what path truly calls you towards it. You may even have found your purpose, your reason for making these massive changes.

In the end I spent thirteen months travelling through Nepal, Thailand, Australia, New Zealand and Western America and this had a massive impact on my life. This was because I had put myself into a position where I could learn the universal lessons, I had been teaching others for so long.

I have been through the process you have been through whilst reading this book, the same process I have been supporting my clients to go through for years. I remember smiling to myself on the plane back to England at the end of my travels, as I thought to myself, 'Who would have thought all the tools you have been teaching people for years would work for myself? Doh.' But I was smiling. I wasn't criticising myself for not doing it earlier.

At the start of my travels, I had no expectations, other than wanting it to give me some answers to questions I maybe didn't even know existed. I had completely opened myself up to investing in me, which is what you have done by reading this book and trying the tips. Sometimes the hardest step is taking that initial leap towards something different, stepping outside your comfort zone, looking at things outside of the normal box. I took responsibility for myself at the start of those travels, and that is what you have done by reading this book. You are finally saying my life is mine; I will lead it how I want.

The thing I learnt the quickest was that I may have simplified my practical life (everything I owned fitted into a sixty-five-litre rucksack, I wasn't working, I was on my own and I had no home) but my mind was a long way off being simplified.

My mind was a battlefield; mines were exploding at random moments. I would have an internal sniper that would make me cower behind anything to protect myself from the truth that was trying to make its way to the forefront of my thoughts. I spent days and nights scared of myself, fearful of taking this leap of faith for myself when I should be at home looking after everyone else.

Slowly with each new experience things started to change. The more I simplified the external parts of my life, the more I was reconnecting to my conscious mind. I was being more present in each moment than I had ever been in my life. This was allowing me to take more control, becoming grateful for the big and small in my life.

From the hills of Nepal, I learnt gratitude for what I have and to not always be desiring more. They were the happiest family I've ever met. In my world, they seemingly had nothing but I soon learnt that they had more than most people I know.

I learnt whilst sat at the top of the hill in Pokhara watching the world come alive that I can sit quietly with myself and not be disgusted at what I see but in fact I can be grateful and accepting of the negative things I have done in my life.

I was grateful to the two old washer ladies in Bangkok who taught me to not take things so seriously allowing me to chill the fuck out a bit.

The moments of solitude gave me time to let go of the negative thoughts I had about myself, releasing baggage that I had been carrying for decades.

So many people helped me move forward. The perfect strangers that I met for mere moments in time picked me up when I was down, made me smile when I was sad and accepted me for who I was in that brief moment. The friends I made of all ages and backgrounds, some fleeting, some for life.

I learnt that a second in time with the right person can have a glorious bearing on your path, that a perfect stranger can lift you up when the world seems too much. I am quite sure if I had not gone to Pai in Thailand and met the people there this book would not exist. I learnt to accept my achievements, that it is OK to just be me and that I can take on board kindness.

I became grateful for all the little things, my rucksack, my walking boots, my feet and even my body.

I knew those thirteen months would determine how I lived the second half of my life. Not only had I learnt to live practically in a simplified way but my mind was also so much lighter. The magical process I had been through had simplified my thoughts, leaving me full of understanding and gratitude just for the opportunity to be alive. I was going to continue this path I had risked jumping on all those months before when I nervously got my flight to Nepal.

I remember sitting on the plane back home knowing my life would never be the same again. I knew that if I kept myself open to the universe that good things would come my way. It was exciting times.

The door to the plane opened and there it was: English soil. Just a few steps and I would be back. It was funny because as I was walking down the steps I had no nervous, anxious thoughts, only excitement for what lay ahead.

As I stepped off the last step onto the tarmac, still wearing the same pair of shoes I started with all those months ago, I felt alive, truly alive.

The universal lessons I learnt whilst travelling are everywhere. You do not have to go to the other side of the world to find them. I know this because my life before my travels were full of these lessons, I just didn't consciously notice them or feel it was my time to put them in place.

The clients that came to me had made that conscious choice to put their well-being nearer the top of their priorities so they were therefore in a place to learn the lessons I was teaching. This helped them let go of a history that was dictating their life and allowed them to take conscious responsibility for their own life.

When I made the choice to put my own well-being at the top of the list, my life changed. This is the path you are now on. You should be grateful towards yourself for taking this leap of faith.

As you have learnt already from following the book to this point, all those profound changes can be done wherever your life is in this moment. It takes a desire for **YOU** to be more important in your own life. It takes getting off autopilot and it takes a strength to face down your fears and anxieties.

But trust me, simplifying your mind and being grateful for the world you live in will lead to a fantastic life, full of adventure, joy, and positive energy.

Tip for everyday-

Life is full of people and stuff that we have no control over, stop spending so much time worrying about things you can't change.

YOU must concentrate on what is in your power to affect, which is your thoughts, behaviours and habits. Stop giving your power away so easily, no one except you deserves to oversee your life.

If you still have people and things in your life that don't make you feel grateful for having them there, then go back over previous chapters and simplify them. Taking away toxic influences on your life is paramount, so keep doing what you are doing and you will get there. Gratitude, as with everything this book has shown you, is something to be worked on, you won't get it all perfect straight away. With determination and trust you will.

Task-

I want you to create a new gratitude habit so that over time it becomes something you do automatically without thinking.

Starting your day with gratitude will change how your days are lived so implementing a gratitude moment within your daily routine will help you flourish.

While you're brushing your teeth in the morning or whilst you're waiting for the kettle to boil, take this moment to think of three things you are grateful for that morning. Then go and write them in your journal, this will help you build a reflective tool that shows all the magic that surrounds you.

This can be extended to the evening as well once you have created your new morning routine but don't rush it this is not a race.

You will probably find it easy at the beginning, naming things like the main people in your life, roof over your head. But then it leads to the interesting development of gratitude where you start saying thanks for the little stuff, such as the shoes you wear, the bedding that keeps you warm, the flowers you walk past that make you smile, the shop attendant who is kind and helpful.

Once you start using gratitude regularly you will notice a difference in how you feel during the day, you will become kinder, people around you will become kinder.

Further Reading-

Have a look at the book *The Magic* by Rhonda Byrne, it will support you in growing gratitude for what you already have. It is a great book for creating a new habit of finding joy in the smallest of things.

Universal Lesson #13

Give back to the world.

The final part in the journey is being able to pass knowledge and kindness on to others, giving as many people as possible the tools and confidence to be their true selves.

We are told that we should get something back for everything we do. This is a myth. If you give without the expectation of receiving something back, then the universe will pay you back two-fold in some form.

If you can make giving back to the world your passion or purpose in life then there is nothing wrong with earning a living from it. I have for over twenty years, but alongside that I show kindness and pass on knowledge every day if the opportunity arises.

I am sure some of you will have noticed I have ended on lesson thirteen, this I have done on purpose. Throughout this book I have tried to support you becoming more conscious within your everyday life, hopefully teaching you that just because you have always thought or acted a particular way doesn't mean that must continue.

You were told the number thirteen is unlucky, the person who told you was told the same and so on. This is how our belief systems are built but you now have full control over how you see the number thirteen. The same as you have the control and power of your own future beliefs and behaviours.

Well ladies and gentlemen, it's the final chapter. I expect you have travelled quite a journey since reading the first page. I hope you are feeling proud of yourself, to make this much of an investment in yourself is bloody awesome.

But please don't fall into the trap of believing the hard work is over, because this journey that is life is forever evolving.

Getting yourself to the point in your life where you can teach people the knowledge you have gained is a wonderful place to be but never forget you are always a student of the world. It's hard work keeping in place all the things that you have learnt. You need to keep practising these ideas and techniques to create and maintain an amazing new lifestyle.

When I stepped off the plane on that September afternoon in 2015, I knew I would never live my life the same way again. I knew that part of my own journey would be to continue teaching people about the power they have within them but in such a way that I also flourished.

Me and my new missus, Karen, started a community mental health project in May 2016 which was based in a 100-acre woodland in Kent. Born from both our passions for helping hard to reach groups but in an environment that would bring natural healing and growth to their lives.

Alongside the project I started Woodland Therapy, my private counselling practice. I had always felt the small confines of a sterile office could have detrimental effects on the therapeutic relationship for some, so I took the gamble on moving it outside.

Like I said at the beginning of the chapter it is ok to earn from passing on what you have learnt, this has always been about creating a life well lived. So if you are already in a caring job, or this book has created a passion within you to help others, it is ok for both sides of the relationship to benefit. Then there is the side of giving back where you do it with no expectation of receiving anything back, this can grow into something quite magical.

There is a movement out there called Pay It Forward, this is where we offer an act of kindness to someone with no payment or returned act of kindness. The only stipulation is that the person you are paying it forward to, somewhere down the line does the same.

An example would be the mechanic who fixes their neighbours car for no other reason than they can, no payment, nothing. Then six months later the person who had their car fixed offers their particular skill to someone else, with the same proviso that they pass on an act of kindness in the future.

Suddenly you are creating a community of kindness, knowledge sharing and togetherness.

People start believing that the world isn't such a shit place after all because someone helped them across the road or chatted to them in the shop. You will be amazed at how passing on knowledge and kindness changes the world you live in.

We had our own experience of others paying it forward, when in November 2016 we got a phone call from a neighbour saying the gate entrance to the wood had been vandalised. We immediately drove to the wood that the project was run from, where we found one of the barns we use during the winter was just a pile of smouldering ash. The five containers next to it where we kept our equipment had all been broken into and unceremoniously set on fire. It was a devastating blow after all the hard work we had put in, we didn't understand how a group of people could do such a thing to a community mental health project.

Then something miraculous happened, one of our clients set up a Just Giving page with the aim of raising two hundred and fifty pounds to help buy new equipment. Within two months, over three thousand pounds had been raised, we got phone calls from complete strangers saying we could come to their garages and take whatever we needed to get us started again.

It was a truly humbling and emotional experience for Karen and I, from something so distressing so much good came.

Giving and receiving kindness with no expectations of anything back, is one of the most powerful acts on the planet.

I am hoping that this book and the lessons you have learnt whilst reading it become part of your foundation for life. If at any point you are struggling, go back to the chapter that seems most relevant and use it to lift you back up.

Tip for everyday-

Being able to teach others always begins with teaching yourself first. Never forget that you are a student of life for the small amount of time you are on this planet.

Don't forget that giving back to the world starts with you, be kind to yourself first and the rest will come.

Task-

Is there anyone in your life that would benefit from knowing just one of the universal lessons you have learnt? If so, pass it on, learn to be confident telling people what has worked for you. Maybe they will come back with a universal lesson not spoken about in this book, as there are many, many more.

I want you to write down your skills, your talents and all things that you are good at. It could be DIY, baking, fixing cars, listening to others, being creative, anything that you feel is an ability that someone else would benefit from. Then I want you to offer to do that skill for someone without expecting anything back. Bake a cake for your neighbour, paint a picture for a friend, fix someone's car without charging and so on.

Smile more without the fear of others judging you. Some will, some won't. Don't give them the power to take away your smile.

Offer a kind word to a stranger. The power of kindness is healing to all involved.

I want you to go back through your journal and highlight the things you want to remember. Use this book and your journal as the platform for the changes you want.

Further Reading-

Try and take the time to read *The Alchemist* by Paolo Cohello. It is one of those books that you will read when you are meant to, so buy it, put it on a bookshelf and when you are drawn to it that is the moment to open the first page.

Always remember:

Ordinary people do extraordinary things

every day.

So go out there grab life by the scruff of the

neck and be YOU.

Acknowledgements.

I would like to thank the following people for their support, encouragement, and guidance during the writing of this book.

Karen for always knowing what to say and when to say it. My family for always encouraging my sometimes crazy ideas, it is priceless having such a foundation to work from.

Amber Hatch who treated a first-time writer with kindness and understanding and helped me take an unorganised manuscript and turn it into a much more succinct book, your editing and advice helped me get my book to a place that I was proud of, thank you.

To Anita Wagar for taking on the proof reading of my first book, hope it wasn't too traumatic for you, and Drew Wagar for all the gems of advice around making the book the best it can be, would have been even more confusing without your knowledge.

To Len, Frank, and Peter who I met in Thailand who taught me so much about taking life as it comes and believing in myself. The wild piglets will live on for ever.

To the many strangers who re-taught me the universal lessons in this book. A minute moment in time can make an impact that lasts forever.

Finally, the universe for always having my back, as long as I remember to act on what I already know.

Printed in Great Britain
by Amazon

18303151R00129